Practical C++23 Backend Programming

Second Edition

Crafting Databases, APIs, and Web Servers for High-Performance Backend

Justin Barbara

Published by: GitforGits

Publisher: Sonal Dhandre

www.gitforgits.com

Printed in India

First Printing: October 2025

ISBN: 978-93-49174-56-6

Cover Design by: Kitten Publishing

Disclaimer:

This book, including all its text, diagrams, and illustrations, is an original work developed for educational and informational purposes. The content is not affiliated with, endorsed by, or sponsored by any company, brand, or entity referenced within. All brand names, product names, and trademarks mentioned are the property of their respective owners and are used in a descriptive, educational context only. Every effort has been made to ensure that no copyrighted or trademarked material has been copied or misused in this book. All diagrams and illustrations that are not original have been used with proper attribution and credit to their respective sources.

If you believe that any content in this book infringes upon the copyright or trademark, please contact us immediately at support@gitforgits.com. Upon notification, corrective action will be taken promptly.

Prologue

For me, the release of the first edition of this book was a big stepping stone, both as an author and as a backend engineer who wants to make C++ skills more accessible to everyday developers. The great feedback from readers all over the world, and the comments from professionals, students and teachers, showed that there was a big need for a book that would help people who already know C++ to learn real backend skills. So many readers shared their stories of moving from classroom syntax and algorithm drills into actual backend roles, sometimes for the very first time. They've had a lot of success with shipping APIs, deploying to the cloud, and troubleshooting real production systems, and that's inspired the direction and substance of this new edition.

It's been really successful and the editors have been very helpful. We know some of you were hoping for more in-depth coverage of deployment pipelines, modern containerisation and the nitty-gritty of cloud operations. Those teaching and mentoring appreciated the hands-on structure, but suggested even more emphasis on progressive skill-building and simple patterns to help new concepts sink in. I took all the comments on board and tried to make this edition even more practical for anyone wanting to become a backend engineer.

As you read through the chapters, you'll see that the book is designed with one main idea. It aims to give you the skills, confidence and understanding you need to build and deliver real Backend systems. Each chapter is designed to teach you everything you need to know to get hands-on with writing, configuring, deploying and troubleshooting your own projects. Right at the start, we got stuck into designing APIs and building backend systems. We didn't just stick to the basics, though. We went beyond that pretty quickly and started using modern protocols like gRPC and the key contract-first methods that are now the norm for scalable backend systems.

It's all about building practical caching systems, securing applications with environment-based secrets, and integrating robust web servers. My approach is to show how to tackle testing not as a checklist item, but as a continuous practice that keeps your backend healthy and safe through every iteration. So, when it's time to ship, we dive right in. We're pros at containerization, with Docker's multi-stage builds being a piece of cake for us. And then, we take the plunge into the world of cloud deployment with AWS Elastic Beanstalk. We're all about monitoring and scaling, making sure everything runs smoothly behind the scenes.

In this book, I'm going to share not only what I've learned, but also why I've learned it and how I've learned it. Each chapter is based on real lessons and workflows I've actually experienced. You won't find any of that artificial complexity or esoteric patterns here. Instead, you'll experience the journey as thousands of engineers already have by getting stuck in and bringing modern C++ backends to life, one challenge at a time. I'm really grateful for all the input that went into this second edition, and I'm excited to see you get stuck in. If you're launching your first API, scaling up for real users, or just searching for practical, clear guidance, you'll find a partner and a pathway in these chapters.

Content

Preface

This second edition teaches C++ programmers the practical skills and modern strategies they need to build strong backend systems. All you need is some basic knowledge of C++, and this book will teach you everything else you need to become a backend developer. Each chapter shows you step-by-step examples, real code, and workflows that you can follow to get results. The aim is to make sure you really understand the concepts.

The book starts with the basic structure of backend systems and shows how APIs are the most important way of communicating and how to use high-performance solutions like gRPC to go beyond REST. It will teach you to use, test and improve API endpoints in realistic C++ projects. This will help you to feel more confident in designing contracts first and in real-time data flows. The key parts of the book teaches you to cache things, to make sure your data is correct and to avoid common problems with correct troubleshooting. A big part of the book looks at how to set up and manage modern web servers. It teaches you to use C++ applications with Nginx, SSL, reverse proxies and load balancers in a way that's easy to understand. We then move on to more practical chapters on automated testing, including both unit and integration tests. You get to learn about containerisation, cloud deployment using AWS Elastic Beanstalk, environment configuration, monitoring, and scaling, and all this is taught step-by-step.

The book makes use of simple and clear to teach network programming, how things are set up, and the important patterns that are used in today's distributed systems. While you learn, you please make a note that this edition is focused on practical scenarios and does not attempt to cover highly complex or edge-case architectures.

In this book you will learn how to:

- Learn to design APIs and high-performance gRPC endpoints and services.
- Create and protect backend apps using environment variables, secrets, and strong configuration management.
- Use advanced caching strategies, including in-memory, Redis, and custom eviction for scalable backends.
- Set up and optimise Nginx as a web server, reverse proxy, and SSL-enabled application gateway.
- Use Google Test to perform unit and integration testing.
- Use Docker to create containers.
- Use AWS Elastic Beanstalk to deploy backends into production.
- Use AWS CloudWatch, alarms, and custom log analytics to check the health of apps and resources
- Set up ways to integrate and migrate databases with no deployment errors.
- Keep systems updated, roll back if necessary, and make customizations to respond changing traffic and business demands.

GitforGits

Prerequisites

All you need is some basic knowledge of C++, and this book will teach you everything else you need to become a backend developer. You get to explore the key C++ concepts for backend, various strategies to build backend infrastructure and some of the best practices that makes you smart enough to carry out the app development all alone.

Codes Usage

Are you in need of some helpful code examples to assist you in the programming and documentation? Look no further! Our book offers a wealth of supplemental material, including code examples and exercises.

Not only is this book here to aid you in getting the job done, but you have our permission to use the example code in the programs and documentation. However, please note that if you are reproducing a significant portion of the code, we do require you to contact us for permission.

But don't worry, using several chunks of code from this book in the program or answering a question by citing our book and quoting example code does not require permission. But if you do choose to give credit, an attribution typically includes the title, author, publisher, and ISBN. For example, "Practical C++23 Backend Programming by Justin Barbara".

If you are unsure whether the intended use of the code examples falls under fair use or the permissions outlined above, please do not hesitate to reach out to us at support@gitforgits.com.

We are happy to assist and clarify any concerns.

Acknowledgement

I owe a tremendous debt of gratitude to GitforGits, for their unflagging enthusiasm and wise counsel throughout the entire process of writing this book. Their knowledge and careful editing helped make sure the piece was useful for people of all reading levels and comprehension skills. In addition, I'd like to thank everyone involved in the publishing process for their efforts in making this book a reality. Their efforts, from copyediting to advertising, made the project what it is today.

Finally, I'd like to express my gratitude to everyone who has shown me unconditional love and encouragement throughout my life. Their support was crucial to the completion of this book. I appreciate the help with this endeavour and the continued interest in my career.

Chapter 1: Introduction to Backend Development

As backend programmers, we are part of a continuously evolving story that has shaped how the world communicates, transacts, and innovates online. In this chapter, we set the stage for our entire journey by exploring the dramatic evolution of the web. Understanding this journey is crucial because it demystifies how web applications came to be, and it reveals why backend development is central to powering everything from simple websites to global platforms.

This chapter is our launchpad: we will look at where the web began, how it grew, what shaped its changes, and how **C++** has quietly but powerfully contributed to this progress.

Transformation of Web Ecosystem

Early Web 1.0

Back in the late 80s and early 2000s, Web 1.0 was pretty much static and read-only. Can you imagine a massive library filled with documents, with each page simply connected to the next by hyperlinks?

- Users could click and browse, but not interact beyond following links.
- Servers merely delivered HTML files on request, like no user accounts, no commenting, no content updates except by the site's creators.
- Business and personal sites served as digital brochures and information repositories.

Behind the scenes, the basic web servers (often coded in C++) responded to "GET" requests by pushing files to curious browsers. C++'s speed and resource efficiency made it an obvious choice for Nginx, Apache, and many custom web servers started life compiled from C or C++ sources.

The Web's Journey

The web did not stand still; it learned to move, interact, and adapt.

The Web 2.0 emerged as scripting (JavaScript), databases, and server-side logic allowed web pages to react and update live.

- Dynamic content became the norm as the forums, e-commerce, and personalized dashboards changing the user experience forever.
- C++ began powering backend logic for early large-scale applications, web servers, and database engines requiring high-performance concurrency.
- Social and Mobile Phases introduced real-time communication and everywhere connectivity.

- Social networks, video streaming, and cloud-based applications demanded backends that could scale, handle millions of interactions, and deliver media responsively.
- C++ continued to serve as the engine room for media streaming servers and messaging platforms.

And, then the Programmable Web i.e. Web 3.0 which included the boom of APIs, microservices, and cloud-native architectures.

- Here, the web runs on APIs which are tiny, well-defined interfaces connecting many independent applications.
- The backend systems are highly dynamic and programmable, driven by microservices that can be developed, deployed, and scaled independently.
- C++ finds renewed importance in performance-critical microservices, servers, and real-time decision engines, especially in finance, gaming, and cloud infrastructure.

Throughout this transformation and evolution of Web, the **C++ has been a quiet backbone, most visible in high-pressure contexts demanding raw speed, reliability, and systems integration**. From powering the first web servers and databases to today's cloud-based microservices, the language's evolution has mirrored the web itself: becoming richer, safer, and more modular.

Contribution of C++ in Web's Evolution

As the web transformed, we saw:

- C++ provided the muscle for servers that had to deliver bytes efficiently.
- The database engines (MySQL, MongoDB), network libraries, and protocol handlers are written in C/C++.
- Various C++ frameworks and libraries were adopted to create rapid, asynchronous backend logic for transactions, streaming, and data analysis.

With each language update (e.g., C++11, C++14, C++20, and now C++23), the tools available for backend programming became more powerful and expressive, mirroring the increasing complexity and demand of web platforms. Most critically, **as backend developers using C++**, we enjoy the unique advantage of building at the intersection of efficiency, flexibility, and control.

It allows us to design robust, scalable systems that support the trillions of web requests and interactions that shape modern internet life.

Modern Backend Overview

These days, the backend is often the unsung hero, working behind the scenes to deliver seamless online experiences. **In this topic, we're going to take a look at the architecture and components of a modern backend system, and then show you the crucial functions that backends play in shaping web and cloud platforms.**

Today's Backend Architecture

Most of the modern backend architecture is designed to process vast amounts of data, ensure security, and scale efficiently. And, most web applications are using a layered design, with clear boundaries between responsibilities.

The essential components of such a backend system include:

Server Environment

The server is at the foundation, handling application logic, dealing with client requests and interacting with databases. So, servers are there to listen for incoming HTTP requests, process them, and send responses. They often use frameworks and web server software such as Apache, Nginx, or custom solutions built with languages like C++.

Databases and Data Management

The backend is responsible for the storage, retrieval, and manipulation of data.

- Structured databases (e.g., MySQL, PostgreSQL) are used for transactional data and complex querying.
- Unstructured or NoSQL databases (e.g., MongoDB) provide flexibility for applications with evolving data needs.
- The backend performs CRUD operations (Create, Read, Update, Delete) as users interact with web and mobile apps.

Business Logic and Middleware

This is the "brain" of the web application.

- The business logic layer processes user requests, applies rules, validates data, and coordinates workflow.
- Middleware bridges communication, handling routing, sessions, parsing, error management, and more.

APIs and Microservices

Modern backend architecture increasingly relies on APIs and microservices:

- The **APIs** expose functionalities in a standardized way, allowing other apps and services to interact.

- The **Microservices** split backend logic into small, independently deployable modules. Each microservice handles a specific responsibility, improving scalability and maintainability.

In addition, the backend systems continuously aim to enforce robust security measures, which includes encrypting the sensitive data, authenticating the users, and guarding against the attacks. They also implement optimizations like load balancing, caching, and query tuning to ensure responsive performance as user numbers grow.

Backend Functions in Web and Cloud

If we look at the functions that make the backend such a driving force in today's online world, we can see how important it is. It played the role of:

- Powering Dynamic Content

  Whenever we interact with social media, perform searches, or shop online, the backend manages the logic that personalizes responses, updates content, and orchestrates real-time interactions.

- Centralized Data Control

  All permanent records, like from user profiles to financial transactions are securely stored and maintained by backend systems. They manage complex relationships, enforce access controls, and provide reliable data for frontends and third-party integrations.

- Business Workflow Implementation

  The backend logic interprets business rules, ensures data accuracy, manages state, and applies policies. For example, in an e-commerce setting, the backend calculates discounts, verifies stock, manages shopping carts, and coordinates payment processing.

- Integration Across Services

  The APIs allow multiple applications and platforms to work together. Today's cloud-centric platforms use microservices and API gateways to connect authentication, messaging, payments, and analytics, thereby making online experiences more flexible and powerful.

- Security Gatekeeper

  The authentication and authorization occurs on the backend. We trust backend systems to verify identities, issue and validate credentials, and guard private data against breaches.

- Scaling and Optimization

  The backends automatically scale using containers, microservices, and cloud infrastructure. Caching strategies and database optimizations ensure the response times remain fast, even for millions of users.

As backend programmers, (y)our task is to architect systems that combine all these layers and capabilities for dependable, high-performance web and cloud experiences. The modern backend isn't just an invisible engine; it's the dynamic core of every application's success.

In the coming topics, we'll learn and practice how C++ can help us master each layer. We will explore everything from real-time computation to robust security for advanced backend applications.

C++23 Key Backend Capabilities

Now that C++23 is here, we've got a language version that's been designed to tackle the latest backend challenges. It's all about making it easier, safer and more expressive when building systems that have to handle millions of interactions, automate intelligent behaviours and scale on-demand.

Principles of Advancement

When a developer selects a language for backend engineering, we weigh competing priorities, performance, reliability, scalability, maintainability. C++ has always led in performance and control, but earlier standards sometimes left us writing verbose, error-prone code when facing modern requirements. C++23 bridges that divide: it introduces features that enhance concurrency, simplify asynchronous programming, and even bring introspective capabilities to our toolset.

With every new backend feature or microservice we build, we start to appreciate how each C++23 advancement provides a practical solution for real-world usage. Let's look at these features, their practical sense, and hands-on examples in backend settings.

Executors

All backend systems have to handle lots of requests, from users clicking buttons to machine sensors reporting data. Before C++23, writing thread pools and async schedulers often meant using third-party libraries and writing complex custom code.

Now, executors are a standard part of our workflow. We can build lightweight concurrency models, dispatch tasks to thread pools and scale up without rewriting core logic. So, let's say we're working on a real-time chat server. With executors, we can process thousands of message events, prioritise urgent logic, and offload work to cores efficiently.

Coroutines

The concept of async programming is the heartbeat of backend services, especially those supporting APIs, data streaming, and distributed computation. Early C++ standards provided the foundation; now C++23 enhances it. With coroutines, we can pause and resume computations, ideal for parsing user requests, fetching data, or streaming results.

For example, we are delivering a backend for a news aggregator. So, with the C++23 coroutines, we can accept hundreds of search queries, page through results, and serve data one chunk at a time, without blocking resources or overwhelming memory.

Standard Networking Library

Reliable, secure networking is foundational for today's backend. Until now, C++ lacked a standard approach to sockets, connections, or protocol management. With C++23's networking library, we gain cross-platform APIs to implement HTTP, WebSocket, or TCP/UDP clients and servers.

If we're building a microservice to process orders, native networking features allow secure, modular communication between services, handling requests, errors, and database updates seamlessly within standardized code.

Ranges and Views

Backend code routinely processes vast databases, logs, and transactions. C++23 expands its support for ranges and views. This allows us, as engineers, to create data transformation and filtering workflows that are both readable and performant.

Suppose our backend receives millions of click events every hour. We use ranges to filter by time, transform to metrics, and output analytics without manually iterating or risking off-by-one mistakes.

Reflection

One major friction in backend engineering has always been converting complex data structures to formats like JSON or XML. C++23 introduces reflection, empowering us to inspect types, automate serialization, validate payloads, and even generate documentation dynamically.

We are now able to expose backend models instantly to frontend teams, document endpoints in live systems, and avoid redundant, error-prone boilerplate code, accelerating delivery and reducing maintenance overhead.

std::expected

The ability to deal with errors in a calm and collected manner is a hallmark of a professional backend developer. Before C++23, exceptions were often misused, or failures silently ignored. std::expected lets us build functions that return useful values or clear error states without having to unwind stacks.

For example, there is an order-processing backend needed to check payment, stock and delivery address. Each step returns std::expected, which lets us handle errors at each stage, report problems to users and keep the service running smoothly.

Modern String Formatting

Every backend writes logs, creates analytics reports, and returns formatted responses to clients. C++23's std::format offers a much needed upgrade, removing the risks of buffer overruns and simplifying locale support.

If we develop an audit trail feature for user actions, formatted output becomes both reliable and secure, reinforcing trust in our backend's integrity.

We are no longer constrained by verbose, fragmented solutions. With C++23, we can build systems that are fast, modular, expressive, and future-ready. Each feature is relevant, not only for isolated technical challenges, but for creating real, scalable, and maintainable services that shape the programmable web.

Setting up C++ Backend Toolkit

We're starting on Linux and we want to set up a foundation that gives us fast, reliable and easy-to-maintain backend systems. So, as backend engineers, our environment isn't just a bunch of tools, it's like our lab, library and workshop all rolled into one. The environment becomes a silent partner, speeding up every build, highlighting mistakes, and equipping us with workflows that scale to real-world demands. It is here, in our setup, that lessons learned translate into practical success. A good setup removes distractions. We want to write code and immediately see its effect. We want to test changes, refactor logic, and debug failures without unnecessary friction. Especially with C++23's features, a supportive environment can unlock expressiveness in modules, concurrency, and safety, and ensure projects remain robust for years.

Compiler

We now, at first, begin with the compiler. It is considered to be the heart of backend development. On Linux, the GCC and Clang are the most trusted roads to C++23. The GCC, in particular, is known for its standards conformity and strong optimization. So, when we install GCC using the system package manager, we're gaining a suite capable of turning high-level C++23 code into precise, native instructions for our server.

Following is the system prompt:

```
sudo apt update
sudo apt install build-essential g++-13
```

This installs all core tools needed for complex builds. By specifying a modern version (g++-13 or later), we ensure that there is a support for all C++23 language features.

Just for our verification, we can try running:

```
g++ --version
g++ -std=c++23 -dM -E - < /dev/null | grep __cplusplus
```

This spots the expected output. And, it means that our system is prepared for the journey ahead.

Writing, Exploring, and Debugging Code

Lots of backend engineers like Visual Studio Code as their go-to IDE because it's lightweight but still has all the features you need. When we open VS Code, we install the official C/C++ extension and set up project settings to create a high-productivity environment for our backend apps.

But if we're more into the command line, Vim or Neovim, then it takes time to get the hang of. But once you've got your configuration sorted with completion plugins, syntax highlighting, and smart navigation, it becomes a fast, distraction-free companion. So, when it comes to picking an environment, we should go for one that feels natural, encourages experimentation and integrates with build tools like CMake.

Libraries and Frameworks

To handle things like networking, concurrency, data serialization, or process orchestration, we depend on high-quality libraries. There are powerful options available. The networking function is enabled by Boost.Asio.

Just try the following line to get it installed:

```
sudo apt install libboost-all-dev
```

This gives us access to asynchronous I/O, socket management, and event-driven programming.

For JSON handling, the **nlohmann/json** connects modern C++ containers and classes to web APIs with ease:

```
sudo apt install nlohmann-json3-dev
```

Then, with GoogleTest or Catch2, we can define test suites, validate edge cases, and refactor confidently.

```
sudo apt install libgtest-dev
```

All the libraries should be seen as building blocks. We don't need every option at once, but as projects grow, having these installed means our code can evolve naturally, adapting to new requirements without friction.

Configuring Build System

Many C++ projects are managed with CMake. It orchestrates source files, dependencies, and compilation options. When we write **CMakeLists.txt** files, we actually declare what to build, how to link, and where to find headers and libraries.

```
sudo apt install cmake
```

The CMake is absolutely language-agnostic and multiplatform. With CMake integrated into our IDE, the rebuilding and running of tests becomes effortless.

Final Check

To truly confirm our environment, let's write and compile a small program that uses the latest features.

We create a file named **main.cpp**:

```
#include <iostream>

#include <format>

int main() {

    std::cout << std::format("Welcome to high-efficiency C++
backend development!") << std::endl;

    return 0;

}
```

We then build and run with:

```
g++ -std=c++23 main.cpp -o backend_test

./backend_test
```

If we get the welcome message, then it proves that our setup is ready.

As we develop each module and workflow in the coming chapters, we draw confidence from this high-efficiency setup. We're not distracted by incompatibility or missing features. Instead, we focus on building backend systems that are robust, scalable, and easy to maintain, as every professional Backend engineer should.

Summary

So, in this chapter, we took a look at how the web has changed over time, from how it used to be static to how it is now, which is all programmable. We also talked about how backend systems have evolved to become the hidden engines that make all the digital experiences we use today. We got what backend development was all about and why C++ is so important for creating top-notch, high-performance systems.

When we took a look at the new stuff in C++23, we saw that features like standardised executors, better coroutines, ranges, reflection, and modern error handling really nailed it when it came to solving real-world backend problems and made us more productive. We learned concurrency being safer, data processing more expressive, and communication between services more seamless. Then we had a run-through of setting up a professional Linux-based C++ development environment, picking high-efficiency compilers, editors and libraries that'd be great for fast prototyping and reliable server applications. All these learning experiences have equipped us to confidently develop, maintain, and scale backend solutions prepared for future demands on the modern web.

CHAPTER 2: C++ REFRESHER AND ESSENTIALS

In this chapter, we're going to take a deep dive into the basics of C++ and how it's used in backend programming. We'll start with a practical, hands-on approach to C++ syntax, looking at the building blocks of variables, data types, control flows, and how structure in code relates to real backend operations. Then we get into the nitty-gritty of C++ semantics, looking at the core rules and behaviours, value and reference semantics, move semantics, RAII pattern, and type inference. All of this is vital for writing backend code that's both performant and reliable. We'll be looking at data structures like arrays, strings, lists and vectors, and we'll be finding out how they work and why they're all so important for dealing with and optimising data at the backend.

We'll be looking at the principles and power of Object-Oriented Programming as we learn to design encapsulated, extensible systems using classes, inheritance, and polymorphism. We're moving on to the Standard Template Library now, which shows how containers, algorithms and function objects can speed up coding and problem-solving in backend logic. Finally, we'll look at multithreading, learning methods for running things at the same time, making sure everything's in sync and using resources efficiently. This is all really important for the high-throughput, scalable architectures needed by modern web and cloud backends.

C++ Syntax

It's really important to get the syntax of the language down when we're building a backend system in C++. The thing is, syntax is about way more than just random rules. It's like the framework that helps us express backend logic in a clear, intentional, and confident way. In backend environments, where performance and security are really important, precise syntax is vital for successful code and robust architecture. Every time you declare a variable, write a function or define a control structure, you're essentially making a contract with the computer and with any engineers who'll maintain the system after you. What we've found is that good syntax leads to maintainability, which in backend work translates to fewer outages, easier updates and smoother scaling as web traffic grows.

I'm going to start by building the bones of a backend program. In Linux, every backend service starts out as a **.cpp** file where we include the necessary libraries to handle networking, data processing and concurrency.

Following is a basic structure for a backend prototype:

```
#include <iostream>
#include <vector>
#include <string>
#include <format>
int main() {
```

```
    std::vector<std::string> logs = {"Connected", "User
Authenticated", "Data Saved"};

    for (const auto& entry : logs) {

        std::cout << std::format("Event: {}\n", entry);

    }

    return 0;

}
```

In the above structure, we have included the essential standard library headers. You can explore how the variables and objects are typed explicitly and how the **auto** is used for container traversal. We also have leveraged the **std::format** for safe, formatted string output, as it is considered to be of vital use in backend logging and event reporting.

Variables, Types, and Declaration

We also declare variables to hold every piece of state the backend needs to track, user IDs, session tokens and database connections. Here's an example: a backend that processes purchase orders has to handle integers, floating-point numbers and strings. The point of each declaration is clear:

```
int orderCount = 5;

double balance = 402.50;

std::string customer = "Amit";

const std::string currency = "INR";
```

In the above, the **const** qualifier signals to the collaborators and compilers that a value will not change. Similarly, we can use reference (**&**) and pointer (*****) syntax for efficiency in passing large structures, especially when handling customer profiles or product inventories.

Control Structures and Logic Flow

Most of the experience developers know that the backend app logic demands decision-making, looping, and error handling. Now here, the C++ provides several constructs. For example, if we write an endpoint to update user profiles, we can check the input and branch execution accordingly:

```
if (isAuthenticated(user)) {

    updateProfile(user, data);

} else {
```

```
    std::cout << "Unauthorized access attempt blocked.\n";
}
```

And, in a backend where bulk processing is quite common, then we can easily use loops to carry out the batch operations, such as updating the cached records or parsing the log files.

```
for (const auto& record : records) {
    process(record);
}
```

And, when it comes to backend request types or protocol dispatching, there's no better option than **switch** statements. They make things crystal clear and are super flexible for complex workflows.

Functions

Essentially, large backend systems are made up of specialised functions, request handlers, database operations and utility routines. When we define functions, we make sure to use type-safe arguments and explicit return types.

```
bool isAuthenticated(const std::string& token) {
    // Authentication logic here
    return token == "valid";
}
```

The overloading of functions allows us to tailor behavior based on context. The lambdas and closures, make event-driven and asynchronous backend programming more modular. For example, we might pass a lambda to process a batch of user updates through a queue, capturing necessary state for parallel execution.

Practically, every backend service we build is scrutinized for clarity and correctness through its syntax, because real-world reliability depends on it. As we continue through this chapter, we build upon syntax fundamentals to explore semantics, data structures, and advanced features. It thereby confirms that every line we write is a step toward scalable, maintainable backend excellence.

C++ Semantics

We don't just write C++ for backend systems and make sure the code is organised in the right way. We've got to make a conscious effort to shape the behaviour and meaning of our programs.

In other words, we've got to master semantics. While syntax is all about how you write the code, the semantics is what it does. This includes how variables are set up, how objects interact, and how data moves through your application when it's running. In backend engineering, where reliability and precise behaviour matter most, semantics is what allows our systems to handle unpredictable inputs, manage resources efficiently, and guarantee correctness under load. We, as backend engineers, are entrusted with the business's logic and must ensure our code not only compiles, but also **means** and **does** what is intended as traffic increases and problems become more complex.

Value and Reference Semantics

In backend programming, the way we manage data has a direct impact on the system reliability, scalability, and performance. If you dont know, C++ offers both value and reference semantics. Value semantics means each variable holds its own copy of data, making interactions straightforward and side-effect-free.

For example, when we process user records:

```
User current = db.fetchUser(id);   // Value copy

modify(current);
```

Here, only the copy is changed; the original database record remains untouched until we explicitly update it. This insulation guards against accidental data loss or corruption in multi-threaded environments.

On the other hand, reference semantics provides powerful performance benefits and enable direct manipulation of shared data, sometimes vital when backend processes must update shared caches, metrics, or connection states:

```
void updateBalance(Account& acct, double amt) {

    acct.balance += amt; // Changes reflect outside this
function

}
```

The key to writing correct and efficient backend code is knowing when to use value versus reference semantics. We use value where isolation is important (e.g. batch processing, querying), and references where shared operations are necessary (e.g. session management, resource pools).

Move Semantics and Resource Management

Since C++11, there's been move semantics, which let us transfer ownership of resources like large data buffers or network sockets without having to make expensive deep copies. In backend work, this means our systems can scale to handle large volumes of traffic without bogging down due to unnecessary copying.

For example, assume that we are receiving a batch of HTTP payloads:

```
std::vector<Data> processBatch(std::vector<Data>&& input) {
    // input is 'moved from', function takes ownership
efficiently
    return std::move(input);
}
```

So here, with the use of **`std::move`**, we are signaling that the function can "steal" the input's contents, leaving the old variable in a valid-but-unspecified state.

RAII (Resource Acquisition Is Initialization)

All backend engineers need to keep an eye on resources, memory, files and sockets, making sure nothing is leaked or mishandled. The C++ language has this built in via RAII, which basically means that any resource allocated is automatically released when the owning object goes out of scope. This isn't just a good idea, it's essential for keeping the backend stable, especially when you're juggling a lot of tasks.

For example, if we open a log file as part of user request handling:

```
void logEvent(const std::string& msg) {
    std::ofstream log("events.log", std::ios::app); // Opens
and closes automatically
    log << msg << std::endl;
}
```

The file handle closes when the function completes, preventing leaks and saving manual cleanup code, an enormous benefit for backend systems under continuous stress.

Type Inference and Modern Initialization

Increasingly, the backend code need to be kept flexible and maintainable. With the use of C++'s **`auto`** and structured bindings, we can easily write declarations that can adapt gracefully with the change in data models:

```
auto [user, status] = getUserAndStatus(id);
```

This keeps backend handlers concise, easily refactored, and strongly typed, reducing both bugs and cognitive load.

The whole point of backend development is to use semantics to design systems that are correct, performant and safe. If we understand value and reference semantics, move operations, RAII, and modern initialization patterns, we can keep our web and cloud platforms reliable, responsive, and easy to maintain as complexity grows. If we make clear semantic decisions, we can bring our business logic to life and make sure every request, transaction and data flow works as it should.

C++ Data Structures

In backend engineering, choosing and mastering the right data structures is fundamental. As backend developers, we balance between built-in arrays for speed, **std::vector** for flexible storage, linked lists for dynamic operations, stacks for request management, and maps for fast lookups. If we code each one directly, we'll both understand how they work and be able to make architectural decisions under pressure.

Arrays

The arrays are simple yet efficient for storing contiguous elements of the same type. In the following, we can define and use an array to log HTTP status codes processed by a backend:

```
#include <iostream>
int main() {
    int statusCodes[5] = {200, 404, 500, 302, 403};
    for(int i = 0; i < 5; ++i) {
        std::cout << "Processed status: " << statusCodes[i] <<
std::endl;
    }
    return 0;
}
```

The arrays provide fast indexed access, which helps when we know up front the number of items and need high-speed iteration in backend algorithms.

std::vector

Unlike arrays, the vectors grow and shrink as needed, ideal for unpredictable, high-traffic backend situations like accumulating logs or requests:

```
#include <iostream>
```

```
#include <vector>
int main() {
    std::vector<std::string> logs;
    logs.push_back("Server started");
    logs.push_back("User logged in");
    logs.push_back("Data saved");
    for(const auto& log : logs) {
        std::cout << log << std::endl;
    }
    return 0;
}
```

The vectors handle resizing and memory automatically, which makes them indispensable for modern backend workflows.

Linked List

While **std::list** accomplishes double-linked lists, sometimes we can implement our own for greater control, especially for custom request queues:

```
#include <iostream>
struct Node {
    int data;
    Node* next;
};
int main() {
    Node a{100, nullptr};
    Node b{200, nullptr};
    a.next = &b;
    Node* ptr = &a;
    while(ptr != nullptr) {
        std::cout << "Node value: " << ptr->data << std::endl;
        ptr = ptr->next;
```

```
    }
    return 0;
}
```

This above structure lets us enqueue and dequeue elements efficiently for backend processing.

Stack and Map

A stack is really important for things like handling function calls, changes to the state, or reversing operations in back-end logic.

```
#include <iostream>
#include <stack>
int main() {
    std::stack<std::string> events;
    events.push("connect");
    events.push("authenticate");
    events.push("process_request");
    while(!events.empty()) {
        std::cout << "Event handled: " << events.top() <<
std::endl;
        events.pop();
    }
    return 0;
}
```

In addition, the backend systems also very oftenly requires the rapid mapping of keys to values. One classic example of it is matching usernames to user IDs, or request URLs to service handlers. So here, the **std::map** does provide the fast lookup and organization.

Following is the sample program:

```
#include <iostream>
#include <map>
int main() {
    std::map<std::string, int> userSessions;
```

```
    userSessions["Amit"] = 10;
    userSessions["Neha"] = 21;
    userSessions["Ravi"] = 44;
    for(const auto& [user, session] : userSessions) {
        std::cout << user << " => SessionID: " << session <<
std::endl;
    }
    return 0;
}
```

With every backend feature, we look at how much data there is, how often it changes, and how complicated it is. When you need something fixed and fast, arrays are the way to go. We've got vectors for scalable, sequential data. We've got all the lists you need for flexible chains. Stacks for reversibility. And there are maps for relationships and fast searches. If we code each one and understand their strengths and constraints, we can create backend solutions that are not only robust but also efficient, meeting real-world demands in web, cloud, and beyond.

OOP in C++

Object-Oriented Programming (OOP) is really important for organising code, modelling real-world entities, and building scalable solutions, especially as backend systems start to get more complex. Our backend workflows are created using OOP principles like encapsulation and inheritance, which help us make them modular, easy to maintain and secure. If they're taught in a really practical way, it'll help us represent users, sessions, resources and services as strong objects.

Encapsulation

The concept of encapsulation is the heart of OOP. It allows us to wrap data and the functions that operate on it inside one logical unit. In backend practice, this means representing each resource as an object with private state and public methods.

See the following simple backend user model:

```
#include <iostream>
#include <string>
class User {
private:
```

```
    std::string username;
    int sessionId;
public:
    User(const std::string& name, int id) : username(name),
sessionId(id) {}
    std::string getUsername() const { return username; }
    void changeSession(int id) { sessionId = id; }
    int getSessionId() const { return sessionId; }
};
int main() {
    User u1("Amit", 1001);
    std::cout << u1.getUsername() << " has session " <<
u1.getSessionId() << std::endl;
    u1.changeSession(2050);
    std::cout << u1.getUsername() << " session changed to " <<
u1.getSessionId() << std::endl;
    return 0;
}
```

In the above, by marking **username** and **sessionId** as private, we are able to keep the integrity of data. The only defined member functions are able to alter the internal state, protecting against accidental or malicious corruption.

Inheritance

Inheritance is another importance concept in programming. It lets us define relationships between objects, encouraging reusability and logical structure within backend systems. For example, if our backend handles different user types, we can create base and derived classes as shown below:

```
class BaseUser {
protected:
    std::string username;
public:
    BaseUser(const std::string& name) : username(name) {}
```

```
    virtual std::string getRole() const { return "User"; }
};
class AdminUser : public BaseUser {
public:
    AdminUser(const std::string& name) : BaseUser(name) {}
    std::string getRole() const override { return "Admin"; }
};
int main() {
    BaseUser normal("Neha");
    AdminUser admin("Ravi");
    std::cout << normal.getRole() << ": " << normal.username
<< std::endl;
    std::cout << admin.getRole() << ": " << admin.username <<
std::endl;
    return 0;
}
```

In the above, the **virtual** and **override** ensured that derived objects can change or extend the behavior safely and predictably. This is vital when expanding backend features, such as adding service accounts or managing different privilege levels, without rewriting code.

As we proceed to advanced topics, we must remember these deep OOP principles. They prepares us to model more complex backend entities and workflows for professional-grade, maintainable backend platforms.

Standard Template Library

The Standard Template Library (STL) is a game-changer for productivity and reliability. The STL is a collection of template-based classes and algorithms that solve common backend problems efficiently. It can manage large collections, store mappings, sort, search and modify data dynamically. And by using STL, we avoid reinventing the wheel, speed up development and minimise bugs.

Containers

At the core of STL are containers, which store and organize data in ways that match our backend needs. **std::vector** is used when the number of backend records can grow or shrink dynamically. **std::map** and **std::unordered_map** serve fast key-value lookups, ideal for managing session tokens, routing requests, or indexing user records. For unique, unindexed lists, **std::set** and **std::unordered_set** allow quick membership checks and deduplication.

Following is a concrete example for session management in a backend system:

```
#include <iostream>

#include <map>

#include <vector>

int main() {

    std::map<std::string, int> sessionAges = {{"Amit", 15},
{"Neha", 45}};

    std::vector<std::string> expired;

    for (const auto& [user, age] : sessionAges) {

        if (age > 30) {

            expired.push_back(user);

        }

    }

    std::cout << "Expired sessions: ";

    for (const auto& name : expired) {

        std::cout << name << " ";

    }

    std::cout << std::endl;

    return 0;

}
```

Transforming Backend Data

The power of STL lies not just in how it stores data, but in how it manipulates it. With algorithms like **std::sort**, **std::find**, **std::count_if**, and **std::transform**, we process backend data efficiently.

In the following program, we will search for flagged transactions:

```cpp
#include <vector>
#include <algorithm>
#include <iostream>
int main() {
    std::vector<int> transactions = {500, 200, 4500, 120,
6000};
    auto flagged = std::count_if(transactions.begin(),
transactions.end(),
                                 [](int amt) { return amt >
1000; });
    std::cout << "Flagged transactions: " << flagged <<
std::endl;
    return 0;
}
```

These algorithms work seamlessly with STL containers, letting us write concise, readable, and fast code for complex backend workflows.

Iterators and Function Objects

The iterators allow us to traverse containers uniformly, supporting everything from database synchronization to streaming log analysis. The function objects (including lambdas) enable custom filtering, transformation, and back-end business logic.

In the following sample program, we can anonymize usernames before logging using a lambda:

```cpp
#include <vector>
#include <algorithm>
#include <iostream>
int main() {
    std::vector<std::string> users = {"Amit", "Neha", "Ravi"};
    std::for_each(users.begin(), users.end(), [](std::string&
name) {
        name = "User"; // Anonymize
    });
```

```
    for (const auto& name : users) {
        std::cout << name << std::endl;
    }
    return 0;
}
```

The STL, as overall, is beyond just a toolkit. It is the engine behind scalable, composable backend services that handle thousands of requests, store millions of records, and support evolving web architectures with ease. As we move forward, the STL patterns and workflows become second nature to solve newer backend challenges, and that too with confidence and speed.

Multithreading

These days, backend servers have to handle lots of requests at once, deal with events as they happen and make the most of multicore CPUs. The beauty of multithreading is that it lets us do loads of tasks at once, speeding up data processing, network actions and service logic. For us, it's really important to get multithreading right if we want our systems to be responsive and scalable.

Let's say there's a backend scenario where different threads need to write messages, like when requests are coming in at the same time. So here, we're going to write a C++ program that logs user actions in parallel.

```
#include <iostream>
#include <thread>
#include <vector>
#include <mutex>
std::mutex logMutex;
void logAction(const std::string& user, int action) {
    std::lock_guard<std::mutex> guard(logMutex);
    std::cout << "User: " << user << " performed action " <<
action << std::endl;
}
int main() {
    std::vector<std::thread> threads;
    for (int i = 0; i < 5; ++i) {
```

```
        threads.push_back(std::thread(logAction, "User" +
std::to_string(i), 100 + i));
    }
    for (auto& t : threads) {
        t.join();
    }
    std::cout << "All actions logged in parallel." <<
std::endl;
    return 0;
}
```

In the above example, we defined a **logAction()** function. Each thread runs this function, simulating concurrent server requests from five users. We use a **std::mutex** and **std::lock_guard** to protect the critical section, output to the console, thus confirms that the log messages do not overlap or get mixed up. The **std::thread** is used to launch multiple threads from **main()**, demonstrating parallel execution. The **join()** call ensures the program waits for all threads to finish before completing, mirroring practical backend processes where we must keep services alive until all work is processed.

This simple case resembles logging or recording events from simultaneous users on a backend web server, processing HTTP requests, updating shared resources, or handling real-time notifications.

Summary

So, we got to better understand the main parts of C++ that apply to backend programming. We learnt how to use C++ syntax really well, and we found out how variables, types, functions and control structures work together to define backend workflows and keep things clear for the compiler and our collaborators. We looked into how to use semantics better, how to tell the difference between value and reference usage, how to use move semantics, and how to make sure resources are safe by using RAII.

Then we moved on to arrays, vectors, linked lists, stacks and maps, which got us ready to design efficient, responsive storage for backend data. For object-oriented programming, we used encapsulation and inheritance, and set up the backend entities to be modular, easy to maintain and extend. And the Standard Template Library really helped with that, as it let us manage and transform data collections using containers, algorithms, and iterators. At last, we made multithreading a reality with a hands-on programme. We used threads and mutexes to process requests at the same time and protect shared resources. In the process, we picked up some great techniques to make sure our systems could handle more work and were reliable when things got more complicated.

CHAPTER 3: DEEP DIVE INTO ALGORITHMS

Algorithms Overview

In backend systems, the algorithms are like the hidden engines that make everything work. They decide how quickly we can sort millions of transactions, search for specific users, make the most of our resources and solve tricky problems like load balancing or planning routes. The right algorithms can help us write code that uses resources well, is easy to predict and can be scaled up or down as needed. So, from handling requests and managing data to scheduling jobs and dealing with database queries, we used simple, effective algorithms to make sure everything was running smoothly. Each time our system responded straight away to a web request or handled a surge in traffic, we saw the real-world impact of choosing and implementing the right algorithms.

As a backend engineer, we never just start coding an algorithm without knowing what we're doing. The first thing we need to do is define the problem, its inputs and outputs, and the constraints of the architectural context. We need to decide whether speed or memory is more important. Was the data sorted or unsorted? We need to work out if each microservice needs its own workflow, or if we can reuse common patterns.

A typical backend algorithm design generally looks like the below:

1. **Problem Definition** in which what the backend needed to solve, must be clarified correctly (e.g., searching for a user, sorting payments).
2. **Inputs and Outputs** is concerned about the data the algorithm accepted and the result it produced need to be specified, for example, an array of records and a sorted output.
3. **Stepwise Process** breaks down the workflow into actionable steps (e.g., comparison, partitioning, recursion).
4. **Optimization** is also needed which focus upon reducing time or space complexity and leveraging better data structures with the backend scaling.

In the next couple of topics, we will get into specialized aspects like sorting, searching, graphs, hashing, recursion, iteration, and dynamic programming. And, we will explore each of them with sample problems and working code in our project context.

Algorithm Design

A good algorithm is the key to making sure your backend systems work perfectly or not. Basically, if algorithms are the engines, then design is the blueprint. We map out what we want to accomplish, how we're going to achieve it, what resources we'll need, and how we'll handle edge cases and failures. So, backend programming is all about designing clear algorithms, picking the right data structures, and optimising for both speed and space, while keeping an eye on the platform's limits.

To start with, we asked, "What exactly is my backend supposed to do?" For example, if we've got thousands of products that need updating, our algorithm design needs to specify how to search, sort and update efficiently, while keeping things consistent in concurrent environments.

Backend Algorithm Design Steps

The design of backend algorithms generally begins with:

- clarifying inputs and outputs. Here, we define what data enters the system and what must be produced. For example, the user requests that trigger database updates or generate page recommendations.
- Next, we break down the solution by dividing problems into sequenced sub-tasks, often combining sorting, searching, or recursive processes to build a complete solution.
- We then select data structures, choosing arrays, vectors, maps, or trees based on their fit to the specific backend scenario and access patterns.
- And finally, we account for scale by considering how the logic performs as data volume grows, when edge cases occur, or within concurrent systems.

Order Processing Backend Design

If our backend has to deal with new orders, updating inventory and confirming payments, then that's a lot to look after. So here, the input will be the list of orders, and that too each of them with product ID and quantity.

Now here, the process will be:

- Search inventory for product.
- Confirm sufficient stock.
- Update quantity.
- Log outcome.

The desired output will be the updated inventory and the confirmation messages. The following is a simplified code block capturing the core of such a design:

```
#include <iostream>
#include <unordered_map>
#include <vector>
struct Order {
    std::string productId;
    int quantity;
};
```

```
int main() {
    std::unordered_map<std::string, int> inventory {{"A1",
20}, {"B2", 50}};
    std::vector<Order> orders = {{"A1", 5}, {"B2", 10}};

    for(const auto& order : orders) {
        if (inventory[order.productId] >= order.quantity) {
            inventory[order.productId] -= order.quantity;
            std::cout << "Order processed for " <<
order.productId << std::endl;
        } else {
            std::cout << "Stock insufficient for " <<
order.productId << std::endl;
        }
    }
    return 0;
}
```

We will then test the solution, in which we will check for both normal and edge cases, in order to understand what happened when stock was low or records were missing, and to verify if the outcomes were logged correctly. This design and testing phase has always yielded a robust, efficient services that could handle real business pressure and deliver results accurately, every time.

Sorting Algorithms

All backend systems are built on ordered data, transactions, messages, logs, search results and more. This is where sorting algorithms come in. They bring structure to chaos, enabling fast searches, reliable reporting, and efficient resource management. The backend servers can handle millions of records in a flash, so they're super quick to respond to client requests and keep everything in sync as use increases.

If we pick the right sorting algorithms, we can turn loads of data into easy-to-use information. We need both speed and scalability in backend applications, and often our sorting logic supports other algorithms such as searching or batching.

Let's examine a practical implementation of one of the most relevant sorting algorithms, **Quick Sort**, and then we will learn about the other sorting methods, and how they are appropriate for backend tasks.

Quick Sort

The **Quick Sort** is one of the fastest sorting algorithms in practice, especially for large, unsorted arrays encountered in backend systems. It divides the array into partitions around a pivot, recursively sorting each side.

Following is a sample C++ implementation to sort an array of user IDs:

```
#include <iostream>
#include <vector>
int partition(std::vector<int>& arr, int low, int high) {
    int pivot = arr[high];
    int i = low;
    for (int j = low; j < high; j++) {
        if (arr[j] < pivot) {
            std::swap(arr[i], arr[j]);
            i++;
        }
    }
    std::swap(arr[i], arr[high]);
    return i;
}
void quickSort(std::vector<int>& arr, int low, int high) {
    if (low < high) {
        int pi = partition(arr, low, high);
        quickSort(arr, low, pi - 1);
        quickSort(arr, pi + 1, high);
    }
}
int main() {
```

```
    std::vector<int> userIds = {42, 106, 7, 92, 55};
    quickSort(userIds, 0, userIds.size() - 1);
    std::cout << "Sorted userIds: ";
    for (const auto& id : userIds) {
        std::cout << id << " ";
    }
    std::cout << std::endl;
    return 0;
}
```

This algorithm sorts the IDs quickly. It guarantees that the backend components can process, display, or index users efficiently.

STL std::sort

For real backend C++ systems, we often use the STL's built-in sort for convenience and reliability:

Following is a sample implementation of **`std::sort`**:

```
#include <algorithm>
#include <vector>
#include <iostream>
int main() {
    std::vector<int> values = {14, 8, 21, 3};
    std::sort(values.begin(), values.end());
    for (int v : values) std::cout << v << " ";
    std::cout << std::endl;
    return 0;
}
```

This particular algorithms is well optimized and tested. It is quite a go-to algo for most backend needs unless specialized sorting is required.

There are other algorithms such as:

- **Bubble Sort,** which is only used for very small lists or when teaching sorting principles.

- **Merge Sort** is preferred for large datasets on systems where stable sorting and out-of-place merging matter, useful on backend file or database merges.
- **Heap Sort** comes into play for priority queue applications, like job scheduling in backend processors.

Once we understand and put these sorting algorithms in place, we can then only make the backend servers able to organise and process huge amounts of data to have the services predictable, reliable, and easy for users to get on.

Search Algorithms

Frequently, backend services need to look up user profiles, validate session tokens, check inventory status, or locate logs and transactions in massive datasets. The way we search for things is like a fast way to find what we are looking for, so that the answers to your questions are quick and reliable.

Which one we choose is really important. If we are dealing with small datasets or sequential logs, a linear search might be enough. But if your data is sorted or indexed, a binary search is way faster, with an O(log n) lookup time. When it comes to web-scale systems, hashing tables make constant-time searches a breeze, which is perfect for backend session management or cache retrieval.

The following is a simple binary search for a sorted list of user IDs, which is very common in backend authentication routines:

```
#include <iostream>
#include <vector>
#include <algorithm>
bool binarySearch(const std::vector<int>& data, int target) {
    int left = 0, right = data.size() - 1;
    while (left <= right) {
        int mid = left + (right-left)/2;
        if (data[mid] == target) return true;
        else if (data[mid] < target) left = mid + 1;
        else right = mid - 1;
    }
    return false;
```

```
}
int main() {
    std::vector<int> userIds = {7, 42, 55, 92, 106};
    std::sort(userIds.begin(), userIds.end()); // Data must be
sorted
    int searchId = 55;
    if(binarySearch(userIds, searchId)) {
        std::cout << "User found: " << searchId << std::endl;
    } else {
        std::cout << "User not found." << std::endl;
    }
    return 0;
}
```

This algorithm warranties for fast queries, which is very vital for performance-sensitive endpoints.

When we find the backend search slowing down as data grows, we need to check first if the data is sorted and if binary search applies. If we are working with dynamic or unsorted datasets, then try using hash maps with open addressing or chaining. And for distributed backends, it's worth thinking about indexing strategies and database-level optimisations, like B-trees.

Graph Algorithms

These days, the backend platforms are also dealing with all sorts of interconnected data, user relationships, network routing, dependencies among services, and mapping paths through data flows. So here, we can use **graph algorithms** to model these scenarios using nodes (entities) and edges (relationships) to solve problems like shortest path, connectivity, network flow, and reachability.

The graph-based thinking is really important for all sorts of backend work, like building recommendation systems, social networks, messaging platforms, service orchestration and traffic optimisation. For example, say we have got a backend routing system that needs to work out the shortest path between servers (nodes). This is where Dijkstra's algorithm comes in. It's a classic tool for this, offering clarity and efficiency for weighted, connected graphs.

The following is a simplified implementation using adjacency lists:

```
#include <iostream>
#include <vector>
#include <queue>
#include <utility>
#include <limits>
const int INF = std::numeric_limits<int>::max();
void dijkstra(int start, const
std::vector<std::vector<std::pair<int,int>>>& graph,
std::vector<int>& dist) {
    dist.assign(graph.size(), INF);
    dist[start] = 0;
    std::priority_queue<std::pair<int,int>,
std::vector<std::pair<int,int>>, std::greater<>> pq;
    pq.push({0, start});
    while (!pq.empty()) {
        auto [cost, u] = pq.top(); pq.pop();
        if (cost > dist[u]) continue;
        for (auto [v, weight] : graph[u]) {
            if (dist[v] > dist[u] + weight) {
                dist[v] = dist[u] + weight;
                pq.push({dist[v], v});
            }
        }
    }
}
int main() {
    // sample graph: node 0 connected to node 1 (weight 5),
node 2 (weight 10)
    std::vector<std::vector<std::pair<int,int>>> graph = {
        {{1,5},{2,10}}, // node 0
```

```
        {{2,2}},        // node 1
        {{}}            // node 2
    };
    std::vector<int> dist;
    dijkstra(0, graph, dist);
    for (int i = 0; i < dist.size(); ++i) {
        std::cout << "Distance from 0 to " << i << ": " <<
dist[i] << std::endl;
    }
    return 0;
}
```

With this type of algorithm, we make fast routing choices, ensure service reachability, and optimize backend traffic in real time.

If the graph algorithms seem slow or memory-intensive for large backend datasets, we can make use of adjacency lists over adjacency matrices, or we can apply lazy loading of nodes, or maybe we leverage libraries like Boost Graph for production-grade performance.

Hash Algorithms

The **hash algorithms** are at the heart of fast lookup tables, caches, and even security solutions in backend environments. When we turn data into fixed-size values called hashes, we make it so that we can access it super quickly, avoid collisions and validate the data. All of this is important for managing sessions, storing passwords and doing quick searches.

So, every time we store user session tokens, retrieve key-value pairs, or detect data changes for synchronisation, we need to use hashing.

Lets have a go at building a basic hash table to manage backend session tokens using C++'s standard library. So, let's say a bunch of users log in, and our backend has to store and check session keys for quick authentication.

```
#include <iostream>
#include <unordered_map>
#include <string>
#include <random>
```

```
// Generate a pseudo-random session token
std::string generateToken(int userId) {
    std::string base = "user" + std::to_string(userId);
    std::hash<std::string> hasher;
    size_t hashValue = hasher(base);
    return std::to_string(hashValue);
}
int main() {
    std::unordered_map<std::string, std::string> sessionTable;
    // Suppose these are logins from user IDs 101, 202, and
303
    for (int userId : {101, 202, 303}) {
        std::string token = generateToken(userId);
        sessionTable[token] = "active";
        std::cout << "Session token for user " << userId << ":
" << token << std::endl;
    }
    // Backend lookup for an incoming session
    std::string inputToken;
    std::cout << "Enter token to check session: ";
    std::cin >> inputToken;
    if (sessionTable.find(inputToken) != sessionTable.end()) {
        std::cout << "Session is " << sessionTable[inputToken]
<< std::endl;
    } else {
        std::cout << "Session not found or expired." <<
std::endl;
    }
    return 0;
}
```

In this example, each user is assigned a session token by hashing their ID with additional strings. The backend stores the token with a status inside an **unordered_map** (which uses a hash algorithm internally) for instant lookup. Every subsequent check for session validity involves searching the hash table.

For higher security or integrity, the hashes are salted and made resistant to rainbow table attacks. If we experience slow lookups or excessive collisions, investigate the hash function's quality, balance the load factor of the hash table, and we can consider alternative hashing strategies suited to the backend workload and scale.

Recursive Algorithms

Recursion allows backend systems to solve problems that have natural self-similarities, such as traversing nested data structures, managing hierarchical resources, and performing divide-and-conquer workflows. It lets us break a large problem into smaller, identical sub-problems, ultimately simplifying code and improving modularity.

Consider a backend file service that needs to calculate the total size of all files within a directory, including those in nested folders. Recursion offers a clear and maintainable solution. So here, let us make use of a simplified representation (since a real implementation would access the file system, but here we demonstrate the recursive logic):

```
#include <iostream>
#include <vector>
#include <string>
struct FileEntry {
    std::string name;
    int size; // For files, size in KB; for directories, -1
    std::vector<FileEntry> children;
};
int getTotalSize(const FileEntry& entry) {
    if (entry.size >= 0) return entry.size; // Base case: this
is a file
    int sum = 0;
    for (const auto& child : entry.children) {
        sum += getTotalSize(child); // Recursive call for each
child
```

```
    }
    return sum;
}
int main() {
    FileEntry root = {"root", -1, {
        {"file1.txt", 10, {}},
        {"dir1", -1, {
            {"file2.txt", 20, {}}
        }},
        {"file3.txt", 15, {}}
    }};
    std::cout << "Total directory size: " <<
getTotalSize(root) << " KB" << std::endl;
    return 0;
}
```

In the above, each **FileEntry** can represent either a file or a directory (if **size == -1**). For directories, we sum the sizes of all children recursively until we have only files left (base case). For intensive production use, monitor resource usage and test boundary cases to avoid unexpected failures as data or request size grows.

Iterative Algorithms

There are loads of backend routines that use iterative algorithms, like for processing records, crawling logs, analytics and managing workflows. Simply put, the process of iteration involves repeating steps in a loop until a condition is met. This pattern is easy to understand and often more efficient than recursion for large, flat data sets.

So here, let us say that the server logs are too numerous to process all at once. And, they need to be handled page-wise (say, 100 entries at a time). So here, the iterative logic gives us fine control while conserving memory as shown below:

```
#include <vector>
#include <iostream>
#include <string>
```

```
int main() {
    std::vector<std::string> logs;
    // Simulate 350 log entries
    for(int i = 1; i <= 350; ++i) {
        logs.push_back("Log #" + std::to_string(i));
    }
    const int PAGE_SIZE = 100;
    for (int page = 0; page < (logs.size() + PAGE_SIZE - 1) /
PAGE_SIZE; ++page) {
        int startIdx = page * PAGE_SIZE;
        int endIdx = std::min((page + 1) * PAGE_SIZE,
(int)logs.size());
        std::cout << "Processing log page " << (page + 1) <<
std::endl;
        for(int i = startIdx; i < endIdx; ++i) {
            // Simulated processing: could be parsing,
indexing, etc.
            std::cout << logs[i] << std::endl;
        }
    }
    return 0;
}
```

This design breaks a huge log into manageable chunks for monitoring, audit, or further analysis. It is practical, scalable, and avoids resource exhaustion. And, there is a common hack in backend iteration. It is to batch updates, inserts, or notifications for database/API efficiency. It reduces the round-trips and improves the throughput.

Dynamic Programming Algorithms

What's dynamic programming (DP)? Basically, it's a way of getting backend systems to solve problems by making a series of decisions while keeping track of the subproblems that overlap. The DP is often the best choice whenever backend applications need optimising, costing cut or constraints balanced over time. It replaces brute-force recursion with smart caching, which lets us transform exponential-time challenges into efficient polynomial solutions.

The DP comes up with handy solutions for backend tasks like job scheduling, resource allocation, cache maximisation, and predictive analytics, where you can reuse previous computed results to save computation.

Memoized Fibonacci for Resource Forecasting

I'm going to start with a classic example, showing how we go from naive recursion to DP using memoisation. In backend engineering, you could use this approach to predict how much work there'll be or plan regular events.

```
#include <iostream>
#include <vector>
int fib(int n, std::vector<int>& memo) {
    if (n <= 1) return n;
    if (memo[n] != -1) return memo[n];
    memo[n] = fib(n-1, memo) + fib(n-2, memo);
    return memo[n];
}
int main() {
    int n = 10;
    std::vector<int> memo(n+1, -1);
    std::cout << "Fibonacci(" << n << ") = " << fib(n, memo)
<< std::endl;
    return 0;
}
```

In the above, the **memo** vector stores computed results, because of which, each Fibonacci number is calculated only once, and thereby turning an exponential algorithm into linear.

Tabulated Coin Change Optimization

These backend systems often need to make the most of their resources, like using less storage space, balancing loads or splitting payments. I find tabular DP (bottom-up) works really well for these sorts of tasks. We're going to design an algorithm to work out the minimum number of coins you need for a given amount using a set of denominations.

```
#include <iostream>
```

```
#include <vector>
#include <climits>
int coinChange(const std::vector<int>& coins, int amount) {
    std::vector<int> dp(amount + 1, INT_MAX);
    dp[0] = 0;
    for (int coin : coins) {
        for (int x = coin; x <= amount; ++x) {
            if (dp[x - coin] != INT_MAX) {
                dp[x] = std::min(dp[x], dp[x - coin] + 1);
            }
        }
    }
    return dp[amount] == INT_MAX ? -1 : dp[amount];
}
int main() {
    std::vector<int> coins = {1, 2, 5};
    int amount = 11;
    int minCoins = coinChange(coins, amount);
    if (minCoins != -1)
        std::cout << "Minimum coins for " << amount << " = "
<< minCoins << std::endl;
    else
        std::cout << "No solution exists." << std::endl;
    return 0;
}
```

In the above, we are filling a **dp** table from the smallest target (0) upwards, which is always reusing earlier computed results for the fastest calculation. For backend microservices dealing with billing or logistics, it ensures optimal results with high efficiency.

Longest Increasing Subsequence for Predictive Analytics

We all know it's common practice to try and predict trends or relationships in backend data, and DP is great at finding the most efficient pattern. So, let's see if we can work out the longest increasing subsequence in this array. This is pretty useful for things like ranking, event prediction and analytics.

```
#include <iostream>
#include <vector>
#include <algorithm>
int LIS(const std::vector<int>& nums) {
    if(nums.empty()) return 0;
    std::vector<int> dp(nums.size(), 1);
    int maxLen = 1;
    for(size_t i = 1; i < nums.size(); ++i){
        for(size_t j = 0; j < i; ++j){
            if(nums[i] > nums[j]){
                dp[i] = std::max(dp[i], dp[j] + 1);
            }
        }
        maxLen = std::max(maxLen, dp[i]);
    }
    return maxLen;
}
int main() {
    std::vector<int> data = {10, 9, 2, 5, 3, 7, 101, 18};
    std::cout << "Length of LIS: " << LIS(data) << std::endl;
    return 0;
}
```

This above DP solution finds the largest pattern, equipping backend platforms for smarter predictions.

Each DP solution as explained above, replaces the redundant computation with smart state tracking, whether through memoization (top-down) or tabulation (bottom-up). By decomposing complex backend tasks and amortizing work, DP uniquely supports scalable, predictive, and optimized systems, building the backbone of intelligent backend engineering.

Summary

Algoritms are super important for backend problem solving, and we have learned very well how such good algorithms are key to efficiency and scalability. We practised designing algorithms by working out the inputs, outputs and breakdowns, and saw how careful planning led to strong backend solutions. Then we coded and used sorting algorithms to organise transactions, logs and user data, using both Quick Sort and optimised STL routines. We've got search algorithms like binary search and hash-based lookups. We used graph algorithms to solve network routing and modelling relationships, with Dijkstra's algorithm.

Later, we came up with a way to make sure sessions were managed securely and quickly, figured out how to sort out problems with collisions and made advanced hashing work for scaling lookups. We were able to solve all sorts of nested and paginated problems really neatly using recursive and iterative algorithms. Finally, we looked at dynamic programming in depth, using lots of examples to show how memoisation and tabulation can turn complex, resource-intensive backend problems into scalable, optimised solutions for forecasting, payment splits and pattern analytics.

Chapter 4: Mastering Git and GitHub

In this chapter, we're going to get hands-on with Git and discover the tools professional backend teams use to keep code organized, secure, and ready for deployment. The first thing we'll tackle is what makes version control so essential for every serious project, especially when things start moving fast and multiple people are working on the same microservices or APIs. We'll dig into setting up Git locally, running through real workflows for adding, committing, and rolling back changes, and see how branching lets us experiment with new features without putting production at risk.

We'll walk step-by-step through working with GitHub, from opening new repositories to forking, making pull requests, and collaborating on code reviews from anywhere in the world. There are practical demos for merging and resolving conflicts, plus we'll see how Git's tagging, stashing and reverting tools help us manage releases and recover from mistakes before they go live. Along the way, we will get tips for making collaboration with contributors feel smoother, keeping the history clear, and pushing the code to remote servers without a hitch. By doing all this, we'll build up a professional, maintainable workflow to keep growing backend projects organized.

Exploring Git

When we manage backend development, systems quickly become complex, features multiply, bug fixes stack up, and code must stay available for rollbacks, audits, and team collaboration. Version control, especially with Git, ensures every change is safely tracked, letting us experiment, revert mistakes, and keep history clear for every contributor. In addition, version control also means we are never afraid of trying new ideas or making critical updates. Whether it's deploying a new API endpoint, migrating a database schema, or fixing a security flaw, we confidently adjust code because everything is reversible, reviewable, and ultimately recoverable.

And, Git is the backbone of almost every serious backend project, and once we get the hands on it, we will see it's all about tracking and controlling the code. Git works by capturing snapshots of the files every time we commit, letting we rewind, compare, and patch up mistakes without losing a beat.

Principles and Workflow

We start with initializing a local Git repository, commit disciplined changes, push to remote servers, and open issues and pull requests as features or fixes are ready. The repo hosting platforms become our insurance against lost work, our platform for reviewing and improving code, and our gateway for releasing work in a transparent, maintainable fashion. As we move through this chapter, each tool, command, and workflow will be learned with the aim of making backend development safe, scalable, and productive for teams at any size.

Routine Commands

When we kick off a new backend project, the workflow starts with just a few commands:

```
mkdir backend-demo
cd backend-demo
git init
```

Next, we add files, like **app.cpp**, by staging and committing changes:

```
echo '// backend entry point' > app.cpp
git status
git add app.cpp
git commit -m "Initial app skeleton"
```

Every update gets a new commit:

```
# Edit files as needed...
git add app.cpp
git commit -m "Added authentication function"
```

Tracking History

To check what's new, what's tracked, or what's staged, we use:

```
git status
git diff
```

We can get a fast rundown of the commit history:

```
git log --oneline
```

All these allows us to see every change, who made it, when, and what changed. It keeps the backends' evolution crystal clear.

If we make regular commits, we can try out features, fix bugs and even break things, safe in the knowledge that we can roll back or review past work. It gives us the confidence to experiment in development without worrying about making massive mistakes. Every command we use, **init**, **add**, **commit**, **status**, and **log**, brings stable, efficient teamwork. The more we use these basics, the smoother the workflow becomes and motivates us to get into more advanced tricks.

Basic Git Commands and Workflow

In backend development, the workflow is only as good as the mastery of the essential Git commands. They are the daily tools that keep the codebase tidy, let us recover from mistakes, and enable smooth teamwork where everyone can edit, test, and deploy new features without stepping on each other's toes.

We start by checking the current state of the project:

```
git status
```

This shows what's changed, what's staged, and which files are untracked.

Now, to add a new controller file or fix to the backend:

```
git add controllers/payment.cpp
```

We can add multiple files together, or all changes at once with:

```
git add .
```

Once we are ready, we can then commit the changes:

```
git commit -m "Implemented payment controller and bugfixes"
```

To revert:

```
git checkout -- controllers/payment.cpp
```

Or, if we want to roll back the last commit:

```
git reset --hard HEAD~1
```

To see who changed what and when, check the log:

```
git log --oneline
```

For backend teams, regular commits, clear messages, and checking status before every push or pull forms a disciplined, error-resistant workflow. This habit means the project stays ready for anything, hotfixes, rollbacks, and fast pivots as requirements change. As we keep using these commands, we will notice the confidence growing, the project history making sense, and the team catching fewer errors.

Branching and Merging

Well, it's all about branching. It's the secret weapon that lets backend teams experiment, build features, fix bugs and prepare releases without ever endangering critical production code. When we are working on a serious backend project, we are going to have to deal with situations where we can't do parallel work, like when someone's building a new payment service while we are fixing a security bug, and we still need to keep the main site up and running. So, this is where branching really shines. It's a methodical way to set up separate sandboxes within the current Git repository. This way, we can work on different goals without worrying about any conflicts.

The moment we create a branch, Git records a separate line of development that starts from wherever we branch off. It's totally up to us to make changes, add endpoints, rewrite authentication logic, refactor request processing, and so on, as long as we don't affect anything that's already working. This means the team can innovate or patch at high speed, knowing the main branch (often called **main** or **master**) is safe for rolling out hotfixes and stable deployments.

Creating Branches

Let's roll up our sleeves. In the project folder, run:

```
git branch
```

This shows all the current branches, with an asterisk next to the branch we are on. To start a new feature or bugfix, use:

```
git checkout -b feature/user-auth-upgrade
```

Now, we are on a new branch called **feature/user-auth-upgrade**. The naming standard commonly adopted is **feature/**, **bugfix/**, or **release/**, followed by a clear, hyphenated description. This keeps history organized and makes code reviews straightforward. When we commit on this branch, all changes stay local. If we list branches again (**git branch**), we will see both **main** and **feature/user-auth-upgrade**.

Switching and Comparing Branches

It's common to switch between branches as priorities shift:

```
git checkout main
git checkout feature/user-auth-upgrade
```

The Git saves and restores the state of the project instantly. It allows us to leapfrog between the improvements.

Now, the teammate may build a **bugfix/login-redirect** branch. Now here, both can work independently, reducing risk of overwriting code.

So here, before merging, they can compare the work:

```
git diff main..feature/user-auth-upgrade
```

This shows exactly what's changed between branches.

Merging Branches

When a feature is ready and tested, we merge it into main:

```
git checkout main
git merge feature/user-auth-upgrade
```

The merging pulls in all changes from the feature branch into main. If changes touched different files, Git merges automatically. If both branches edited the same lines, we will see a merge conflict, marked clearly in the files by Git.

Handling Conflicts

In a big project, there will be some sort of misalignment among teammates. There can be a situation, where both, me and the teammate, both have edited the **auth.cpp**. Here, the Git will highlight the conflicting sections:

```
<<<<<<< HEAD
Original main branch code
=======
Feature branch update
>>>>>>> feature/user-auth-upgrade
```

We review both the changes, pick (or blend) the correct approach, and save the file. And, then we finish the merge:

```
git add auth.cpp
git commit -m "Resolve merge conflict in user authentication"
```

Now here, the best practice is to test immediately after resolving conflicts to avoid accidental breakage.

Stale Branches Cleanup

Once a branch's work is merged, we can delete it to keep history clean:

```
git branch -d feature/user-auth-upgrade
```

If the branch hasn't been merged yet, we can use **-D** to force deletion:

```
git branch -D feature/user-auth-upgrade
```

Also we must remember that, teams often create long-lived **release/** branches where final QA and bugfixes happen before deployment. The urgent changes can go on **hotfix/** branches, which get merged and deployed quickly.

Pull Requests and Merging on GitHub

When collaborating, we generally push the branch to the remote server:

```
git push -u origin feature/user-auth-upgrade
```

After this, we open a pull request from the branch into main. It invites teammates for code review and discussion. The GitHub visualizes differences and flags conflicts, making it easy to collaborate.

But, if a merge gets complicated, we can:

- Use **git log --graph --oneline** to visualize branch history.
- Try splitting large merges into smaller commits.
- Stage the conflicted files before committing the merge.
- Update the local repo (**git pull**) before starting a merge to avoid out-of-date conflicts.

Branching and merging are the backbone of distributed, scalable backend development. Teams move fast, deploy confidently, and maintain order without fear of bottlenecks or loss. Whether we are a solo developer or part of a global team, mastering these tools transforms the workflow, making the backend projects resilient and adaptable in every situation. The right branching strategy lets us innovate, experiment, recover, and deploy at enterprise scale.

Setting up GitHub

GitHub is much more than a web-based code host. It is the epicenter of collaboration for modern backend teams. When we are building APIs, microservices, or distributed systems, we need a place to safely store, review, and deploy code across teams and time zones. GitHub fits this need perfectly, giving us not just remote backups, but also integrated pull requests, issues, and automated workflows for continuous improvement.

Connecting Backend Project

Supposedly we have so far made a simple REST API for handling transactions. Now, we want everyone on the team to work together, push changes, and review code in real time. And, that too, all without worrying about overwriting anyone's work.

Create GitHub Repository

We first head over to https://github.com and sign in or sign up. After this, we then click "New" to create a fresh repository.

Then, we name the repo, as **`my-backend-service`** and add a description. And, then we choose "Private". Now here, we don't need a README yet.

After this, click "Create repository" and the GitHub will show instructions for pushing an existing repo.

Project Linking

In the project directory, which was already initialized with **`git init`**, here we set the remote URL:

```
git remote add origin https://github.com/your-username/my-backend-service.git
```

This now tells the Git where to push the code.

Push to GitHub

We then send everything to the remote server:

```
git push -u origin main
```

If the branch is called **`master`**, substitute that. Authenticate with the GitHub credentials or a token.

After this, we then check the GitHub, the code will now be online, safely backed up, and visible to the team.

Sync, Review and Deploy

The teammates can now clone the repository:

```
git clone https://github.com/your-username/my-backend-service.git
```

Whenever we finish a new backend feature, push to the remote:

```
git add .
git commit -m "Implement payment endpoint"
git push
```

Others pull the latest with:

```
git pull
```

Managing Branches and Pull Requests

Suppose we are adding a new analytics API:

```
git checkout -b feature/analytics-api
git add analytics.cpp
git commit -m "Add analytics API"
git push -u origin feature/analytics-api
```

On GitHub, we will see an option to "Compare & pull request", open that, describe the change, and teammates can review, comment, or approve. This workflow ensures quality and helps catch bugs before merging.

The bugfixes, hotfixes, and releases work in the same way. They make a dedicated branch, commit and push changes, and then open a pull request.

Issues and Actions

Then we can create issues for bugs, like "Login API throws 500 errors", for feature requests, like "Add paginated results for analytics", or for general improvements. Here, we can attach commits to each issue to keep things clear and tidy.

And the GitHub Actions automate backend tasks. We can set up CI/CD to run unit tests on every push, build Docker images, or deploy to cloud servers. These actions are triggered by pushes, pull requests or external triggers.

Troubleshooting

If a push fails, we can use **`git status`** and **`git pull`** to sync up, merge local changes if needed and push again. For sensitive backend keys, we can always add **`.env`**, config files, or any credentials to **`.gitignore`** so they never end up in the repo.

Here, we can also set up the branch protection and required reviews on GitHub for safe deployments, and check audit logs for any important changes or rollbacks.

Repositories, Forking and Pull Requests

The repo are at the heart of the backend project's collaboration and history. It is a very structured workspace linked to the cloud, holding every commit, branch, issue, and change discussion. For our backend API, we set up the repo once and the whole team works from it, syncing, branching, and submitting updates as the project grows.

Forking

Suppose we want to add a major feature, but we are not ready to risk breaking the main version. Forking lets us clone the repository under the own account, where we can experiment in isolation. For open-source backend libraries or APIs, others fork to propose improvements, troubleshoot bugs, or adapt code for their needs.

On GitHub, this is a one-click process. We just have to hit the "Fork" on the repo page, and we get a personalized copy. We can then clone it to the machine by:

```
git clone https://github.com/your-username/my-backend-
service.git
```

Pull Requests

Assuming that in our project, we have finished an analytics dashboard. And, we want to integrate this change with the main repo. But, let us say that the teammates need a chance to review it. SO here:

- Push the branch to GitHub:

```
git push -u origin feature/analytics-dashboard
```

On GitHub, click "Compare & pull request." Fill out a clear title and description: "Analytics dashboard showing live user traffic." The team then reviews the code, leaves comments, and (if all's well) merges it into the main branch. The pull requests allow for code review, automated testing (via GitHub Actions), and a clean history.

Repo Settings

On the repo's "Settings" page, we then enable the branch protection rules. It requires pull requests for merges to **main**, or designating reviewers before changes go live. This protects against accidental deployment of buggy code and ensures every update is properly vetted. After this, we then set up the "Collaborators & teams" so contributors get correct permissions, read, write, or admin, depending on their role in our backend system.

Real-World Workflow

So here, the workflow is as:

- We first create issues for features like "Add JWT authentication," "Paginate results for **/transactions**", and then we assign them to teammates.
- After this, each teammate creates a branch, codes their feature, pushes to GitHub, and opens a pull request.
- And, the reviewers approve. The automated tests are run, and once everything's solid, the branch is merged into **main** for deployment.

So, when new developers join, they fork the repo, contribute improvements or fixes, and open pull requests.

Tagging, Stashing, and Reverting Changes

Sometimes, the working on a backend system means juggling releases, debugging major issues, or pausing mid-task when priorities shift. That's when Git's advanced commands, tagging, stashing, and reverting, save enormous effort and keep the project under control. They let us bookmark releases, shelve unfinished code, and recover from mistakes without losing progress or breaking the system.

Tagging Releases and Major Changes

When the backend APIs hit stable points, version upgrades, big deployments, or compliance milestones, we can tag the commits as a permanent marker:

```
git tag v1.0.0

git tag -a v2.0.0 -m "Second major release with analytics
endpoint"
```

Now here, the tags are visible in GitHub. They make it easy to roll back or audit releases. SO, when we are deploying, we can fetch the exact version we need:

```
git checkout v2.0.0
```

We can keep the tags descriptive and match project versioning (**`v1.1.2`**, **`production`**, **`rc-2025-11-02`**) for easy reference.

Stashing

Now, there may be a situation wherein, we are halfway through coding a new search optimization, and a sudden hotfix for the tagging API jumps in. Than here, instead of the commit unfinished work, we simply stash it:

```
git stash
```

We then fix the urgent bug:

```
# make the hotfix, commit and push...
```

After this, we then return to the stashed changes:

```
git stash pop
```

If we have multiple stashes, we list them:

```
git stash list
```

Then, we apply a specific stash:

```
git stash apply stash@{1}
```

This really works and great for handling interruptions, switching context, or pausing experimental work without cluttering the commit log.

Reverting and Resetting

The mistakes are very frequent to happen across different stages like the backend work, schema changes, API misconfigurations, or accidental deletions. So here, if we want to undo a specific commit, without losing subsequent changes:

```
git revert <commit-hash>
```

This creates a new commit that undoes the targeted change.

But, if we want an immediate resets:

```
git reset --hard HEAD~1
```

This is used very sparingly, and primarily for rolling back uncommitted local changes or for the purpose of cleaning up after botched merges.

All these methods administers that releases are tracked, interruptions don't cost us work, and mistakes are easily corrected, all while keeping the history organized and the system ready for production at any stage. These commands make the difference between fragile projects and resilient, continuously improving backend teams.

Git Hooks and Automation

The Git hooks are scripts that run automatically at key points in the version control workflow. These scripts let us automate repetitive tasks, enforce standards, and connect the backend's codebase to deployment, testing, or notification systems. The most common hooks are:

- **pre-commit**,
- **pre-push**, and
- **post-merge**,

And, each of the above hooks triggers a different automation.

Setting Up Pre-Commit Hooks

Inside any Git repository's **.git/hooks** directory, we can very easily find the sample hook scripts. We can very easily use them. We just have to rename and edit them to run their own tasks.

So here, let us take an example that we want to run style checks or unit tests every time a backend developer tries to commit code:

```
cd git/hooks

cp pre-commit.sample pre-commit

chmod +x pre-commit
```

We then edit the **pre-commit** and add the following:

```
#!/bin/bash

echo "Running style checks..."

gofmt -l ./src

if [ $? -ne 0 ]; then

  echo "Code formatting failed. Please fix and try again."

  exit 1
```

```
fi
```

After this, every **git commit** will trigger this script, blocking bad code before it hits the commit history.

Automating Deployments

While Git doesn't run the **post-push** directly, we can simply use the GitHub Actions to trigger builds and deployments as soon as the backend code is pushed. These automations can run API tests, build containers, or even update staging servers.

So for example, we will set up a workflow in GitHub Actions, within the **.github/workflows/deploy.yml** file:

```
on:
  push:
    branches:
      - main
jobs:
  build-and-deploy:
    runs-on: ubuntu-latest
    steps:
      - uses: actions/checkout@v3
      - run: go test ./...
      - run: docker build -t backend-app .
      - run: echo "Ready for deployment"
```

This configuration can test the code and can also build the container image whenever the code is pushed to **main**.

Enforcing Commit Messages

The **commit-msg** hook can check every commit message before it's added. Here we can add rules for ticket numbers, tags, or message formatting so we can filter and track changes more easily.

We can do it by editing the **.git/hooks/commit-msg** as below:

```
#!/bin/bash
```

```
grep -E '^(\[JIRA-\d+\])' "$1" > /dev/null
if [ $? -ne 0 ]; then
  echo "Commit message must start with a JIRA ticket reference."
  exit 1
fi
```

Notifying Merges

For this, we can use the **post-merge** hook to ping developers whenever there is a new code landing in their repo. Now, this notification can be a Slack notification, email alert, or a build trigger.

To do this, we can edit the **.git/hooks/post-merge**:

```
#!/bin/bash
echo "Code updated, please run tests."
```

With such automations in place, the builds and the faster feedback enables the development for frequent releases without downtime. This makes every backend push, commit, and merge more reliable, saving manual effort and speeding up the project development.

Troubleshooting

Dealing with Merge Conflicts

It's a bit like when two branches change the same lines of code - that's what a merge conflict is. When it comes to backend development, this is pretty standard when a bunch of people work on the same API endpoint or config.

So, when we see:

```
CONFLICT (content): Merge conflict in app/config/auth.cpp
```

We open the file, and look for the conflict markers:

```
<<<<<<< HEAD
the code
=======
```

```
their code
>>>>>>> feature/login-expiry
```

We then edit as needed to resolve:

```
git add app/config/auth.cpp
git commit
```

After this, we then use **`git status`** for unmerged files and **`git log`** to review recent merges. If things get complicated, we then reset:

```
git merge --abort
```

Or, we simply return to the last good state:

```
git reset --hard HEAD
```

Recovering Commits or Overwritten Branches

If we accidentally deleted a branch:

```
git reflog
```

So here, we find the recent HEAD reference, and then we recover with:

```
git checkout -b branch-name <commit-hash>
```

This is very useful for restoring a lost feature or bugfix in backend code.

Fixing Push Failures and Authentication Errors

There are situations when the **`git push`** throws error. So here, we:

- Check for conflicting changes, and then we run **`git pull`** to fetch and merge remote updates before pushing.
- And, if credentials fail, we then re-authenticate, or we simply configure the SSH tokens:

```
git remote set-url origin git@github.com:your-username/my-backend-service.git
```

Unstaging files

To unstage files before committing:

```
git reset HEAD <file>
```

And, for local, but uncommitted edits:

```
git checkout -- <file>
```

Cleaning up Repository History

If the log becomes unwieldy, then:

```
git rebase -i HEAD~10
```

We simply pick, squash, or reorder the commits for a cleaner project history.

Syncing with Multiple Contributors

When working with backend teams:

```
git fetch --all
git merge origin/main
```

This keeps everyone's local repo up to date, reducing conflicts or surprises later.

Handling Large Files and Sensitive Data

The **`.gitignore`** file is quite helpful for logs, database files, and credentials. If we accidentally commit sensitive info, then we can remove it from the repo:

```
git rm --cached .env
```

We can also amend and force-push:

```
git commit --amend
git push --force
```

And, if the file is very large, we then use Git LFS (Large File Storage):

```
git lfs install
git lfs track "*.zip"
```

All these troubleshooting steps allow any backend team to recover instantly, preserve the progress, and keep the work professional and safe.

Summary

So, we got ourselves set up with some practical Git and GitHub workflows that are specifically geared towards backend projects. We started off by getting our heads around how version control was like a safety net for every code change, experiment and deployment, and saw for ourselves how setting up a local repo, adding files and committing snapshots allowed us to track work with confidence. We connected our backend project to real-time collaboration by setting up GitHub, which lets teammates push, pull, and review code without worrying about overwriting each other's work.

We practised branching to create feature sandboxes and merging to bring parallel work into one deployable main line, and we even mastered the art of resolving conflicts and cleaning up old branches. We used tagging, stashing and reverting to manage releases, pause work and recover from mistakes without disrupting the workflow. And the automation scripts and hooks we were using kept standards high, while our troubleshooting toolkit allowed us to recover lost commits, solve push errors and quickly resolve heavy merge conflicts.

Chapter 5: Managing Database Operations with MongoDB

In this chapter, we're going to get under the hood of what makes backend apps tick, the database. Every feature, every request, and every transaction in the backend depends on keeping data organized, safe, and available. We'll see the choice and setup of the database drives everything from signups to analytics, and why understanding persistent storage, schema modeling, and querying power is non-negotiable for any backend developer. It's not just about saving records, it's about building systems that never lose context, don't crumble under scale, and always recover fast from failures.

We'll jump straight into MongoDB as our practical NoSQL engine, but we won't ignore the classic SQL approach. You'll get a direct comparison, plenty of hands-on Linux commands, and see how to install, connect, and model collections that respond to real business logic. There'll be code for CRUD (Create, Read, Update, Delete), aggregation, indexing, and performance tricks, all wrapped in the context of actual backend projects. Whether we are designing a full-stack app, an API, or microservices, what we learn here will make the systems robust, auditable, and ready for the toughest real-world workloads.

MongoDB Fundamentals

In a backend for, say, an e-commerce site, the database does much more than hold customer info. It tracks order statuses, synchronizes inventory, validates payments, and links products to categories with precise constraints. It enables reporting (how many sales last month?), auditing (who changed a setting?), and security controls (who can access sensitive data?).

The SQL databases (MySQL, PostgreSQL) use structured tables, rows, and columns, enforcing strict types and referential integrity. They shine where we need complex queries, joins between tables, and strong ACID (Atomicity, Consistency, Isolation, Durability) guarantees. Whereas, the NoSQL databases like MongoDB ditch rigid tables for flexible documents, JSON-like collections that adapt quickly to changing requirements. They're great for fast, broad scaling and storing semi-structured or evolving business data. Instead of joins, we often embed related info inside a single document or link loosely by IDs.

For example:

- In SQL, we did store users and orders in different tables, joining them via user_id.
- In MongoDB, we can embed user info directly in the order, or reference it, depending on the review needs and access patterns.

Both systems are reliable due to transactions, journaling and failover support, but SQL is stricter and MongoDB is more agile and easier to use. The way MongoDB is set up with its distributed clustering, sharding and replica sets makes it perfect for handling workload bursts, user-generated content and event logs. You can do all sorts of stuff with SQL too, like multi-table updates, with BEGIN/COMMIT/ROLLBACK. Now, MongoDB has added multi-document transactions for business-critical logic, but most apps rely on atomic operations inside single documents or careful design to avoid fragile cross-collection dependencies.

Overall, if our backend's rules are clearly defined and relationships are important, go for SQL. If the data is dynamic, we want scaling without any hassle, or we prefer native JSON handling with the backend APIs, then MongoDB is the one for you.

So here, we'll dive into MongoDB fundamentals, mapping these learnings directly to our backend projects.

Document-Oriented Data Model

The MongoDB organizes data into documents, not rows, each record is a JSON-like object stored inside a collection (which is similar to a table, but far more dynamic). The schemas are not rigid: we can start with just a user's name and email (**`{"name": "Neha", "email": "neha@example.com"}`**), then later add address, preferences, or nested arrays without migrations or downtime.This document model is a breath of fresh air for backend devs used to frequent requirement changes. If we need to store lists, objects, or even raw blobs for a new API response, this is the place to go. All we need to do is drop them in and then return the structure as it is to the frontend.

Following is an example of a nested documents and arrays having a real "order" record:

```
{
  "userId": "613fd...",
  "total": 150,
  "items": [
    {"sku": "carb-123", "quantity": 2},
    {"sku": "eco-456", "quantity": 1}
  ],
  "shipping": {"type": "express", "address": "Delhi"}
}
```

This schema-less model lets us embed everything needed for a query or UI, minimizing joins and boosting read performance. Our API endpoints can query deeply nested paths, filter by fields, or update part of a document, all with expressive syntax.

Performance Profile

The MongoDB engine was designed for low-latency CRUD operations. We can put indexes on any field, even inside arrays or sub-documents, to make searches, reports and validations faster. The software performs well when a lot of things are happening at once (multi-threaded writers and fine-grained locks). It's all done automatically, so any updates are totally consistent.

The system has really powerful in-memory caching, so we can get millions of records in milliseconds if we use the index properly. It's all about efficiency, especially when it comes to complex aggregations (grouping, sorting, projections). If a lot of people start using the website, it's easy to increase the read and write throughput.

And with bulk inserts, we can either insert or update in one go. You can also do streaming changes via change streams or capped collections. This means we can build real-time dashboards or push updates to clients with minimal lag.

High-Availability Clustering

The MongoDB's "replica set" model gives automatic high availability. In production, a replica set is a trio or more of MongoDB servers, one primary for writes, the rest passively synced as secondaries. If the primary crashes, a secondary auto-promotes within seconds, so the backend APIs keep running without intervention.

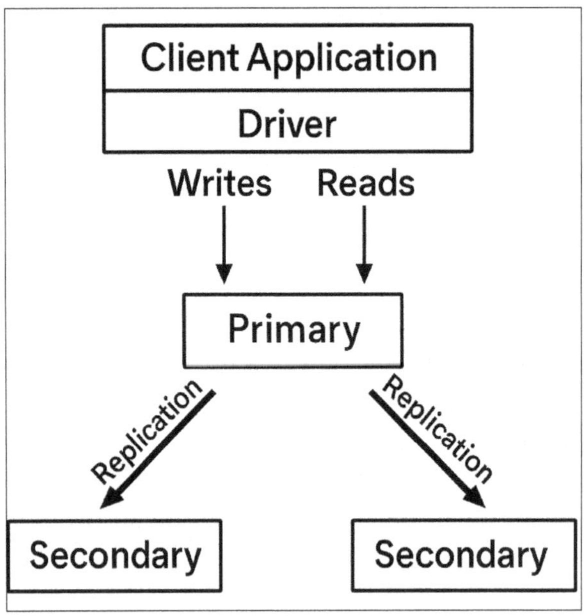

Fig 5.x

Now here, all the writes go to the primary. The reads (if we want) can be balanced across members, making analytics and low-priority work non-blocking on the main traffic. With built-in oplog (operation log), the cluster state is always up to date. Things like automatic failover, self-healing, and point-in-time recovery are major wins for continuous backend uptime.

Scalability

When our dataset grows beyond what one machine can handle, this MongoDB is able to support horizontal scaling via sharding. This means breaking up the collections across multiple servers, each holding only a fraction but working in concert:

- Choose a shard key (e.g., userId, region)
- MongoDB routes data so no single node gets overwhelmed

The sharding keeps API response times low and enables "infinite" scaling, a necessity for volatile workloads and big-data backends.

Real-Time Replication and Backup

The replica sets aren't just for failover, they serve near real-time replication to backup clusters or reporting nodes. The snapshots and continuous backup services (offered in MongoDB Atlas) mean disaster recovery is painless, and auditing sensitive operations is simple.

In summary, the MongoDB is the best fit for our backend project where development speed, flexibility, and scaling are top priorities, and where real business requirements change fast. We can serve, search, and evolve features as rapidly as product needs shift, keeping both backend code and storage agile, resilient, and always user-focused.

Setting up MongoDB

Installing MongoDB Locally

First things first, we need to get MongoDB up and running on the dev machine so we can bring database power to the backend project. The process is pretty straightforward, especially on Linux:

- Import MongoDB public GPG key and add repo

```
wget -qO - https://www.mongodb.org/static/pgp/server-6.0.asc |
sudo apt-key add -

echo "deb [ arch=amd64,arm64 ]
https://repo.mongodb.org/apt/ubuntu focal/mongodb-org/6.0
multiverse" | sudo tee /etc/apt/sources.list.d/mongodb-org-
6.0.list

sudo apt-get update
```

- Install MongoDB

```
sudo apt-get install -y mongodb-org
```

- Start MongoDB Server

```
sudo systemctl start mongod
```

```
sudo systemctl enable mongod
```

Verify the working of it:

```
sudo systemctl status mongod
```

Or log into the MongoDB shell:

```
mongosh
```

- Secure the Instance

Here, we change the default **bind_ip** to allow remote connections only from trusted systems (**/etc/mongod.conf**). And, then we enable the access control and create an admin user:

```
mongosh
use admin
db.createUser({user:"admin", pwd:"supersecret",
roles:[{role:"root", db:"admin"}]})
```

After this, we then restart MongoDB with access control enabled:

```
sudo systemctl restart mongod
```

Local Configuration

Here, we set the environment variables in the project:

```
MONGODB_URI="mongodb://admin:supersecret@localhost:27017/mybac
kend?authSource=admin"
```

Now here, we shall not commit the credentials or config files. We can use the **.gitignore** to keep them private. For testing, we create a separate database (e.g., **mybackend_test**) to avoid polluting production data.

Connecting to MongoDB Atlas

The Cloud-hosted MongoDB Atlas is the preferred choice for production and collaborative backend projects. They offer instant provisioning, backup, scalability, and global distribution.

Create MongoDB Atlas Account

For this, we can go to the https://www.mongodb.com/cloud/atlas and sign up for a free or paid tier.

Create Cluster

We then choose the cloud provider like AWS, Azure or the GCP, and then pick a region and size. After this, we then deploy the cluster (takes a couple of minutes).

Configure Security

Here, under the "Database Access", we create a database user and password. And under "Network Access", we then allow the IP address or **0.0.0.0/0** (not recommended for production!) to connect.

Connect App

For this, in "Clusters", we click "Connect" → "Connect the application" and then copy the connection string:

```
mongodb+srv://<user>:<password>@cluster0.xxxxx.mongodb.net/myb
ackend?retryWrites=true&w=majority
```

We then drop this URI in the backend app's config (environment variable).

Test Connectivity

For this, we can use the MongoDB GUI (MongoDB Compass). Or alternatively, we can test from the code:

```
mongosh
"mongodb+srv://<user>:<password>@cluster0.xxxxx.mongodb.net/my
backend"
```

For this, in the backend, most drivers (Node.js, Go, Python, C++) accept this URI in their connect method.

With the local and cloud workflows established, we can build, test, deploy, and scale backend APIs with seamless migration between the development machine and real-world servers.

Authenticating Backend with MongoDB

The first thing we need to do with MongoDB, whether we are running it locally or in the cloud, is to use connection URIs that always specify the credentials, host, port and (ideally) transport security (TLS/SSL).

Prepare MongoDB URI

For local MongoDB with authentication enabled:

```
mongodb://admin:supersecret@localhost:27017/mybackend?authSour
ce=admin
```

And, for MongoDB Atlas/cloud:

```
mongodb+srv://appuser:password@cluster0.mongodb.net/mybackend?
retryWrites=true&w=majority
```

Now, both these should be injected into the backend's environment variables, and **never** to be hard-coded.

Secure Environment Configuration

In the **.env** or config file:

```
MONGODB_URI="mongodb://admin:supersecret@localhost:27017/mybac
kend?authSource=admin"
```

Or, with cloud:

```
MONGODB_URI="mongodb+srv://..."
```

We add the **.env** to **.gitignore** so the secrets never reach version control.

Initializing Database Client

We now choose the driver matching the backend language. We'll cover C++ (mongocxx), Node.js (mongoose), and mention Go/Python equivalents.

C++ (mongocxx)

Here, we add the dependencies (libmongocxx-dev and bsoncxx):

```
sudo apt-get install libmongocxx-dev libbsoncxx-dev
```

Following is the sample code:

```
#include <mongocxx/client.hpp>
#include <mongocxx/instance.hpp>
#include <mongocxx/uri.hpp>
```

```
#include <iostream>
int main() {
    mongocxx::instance inst{};
    mongocxx::client
conn{mongocxx::uri{std::getenv("MONGODB_URI")}};
    auto db = conn["mybackend"];
    auto col = db["users"];
    std::cout << "Connected to MongoDB." << std::endl;
    return 0;
}
```

This program loads the URI from an environment variable, creates a client and connects to the specified database and collection.

Node.js (mongoose)

Following is the sample code:

```
const mongoose = require('mongoose');
require('dotenv').config();
mongoose.connect(process.env.MONGODB_URI, { useNewUrlParser:
true, useUnifiedTopology: true })
  .then(() => console.log('MongoDB connected.'))
  .catch(err => console.error('Connection error:', err));
```

We adapt the above as same in Go (**`mongo-go-driver`**) or Python (**`pymongo`**).

With a secure connection and working client, we are ready to build robust, scalable backend features, which is powered with a MongoDB database that's safe, accessible, and production-ready.

Schema Design and Data Modeling

We must know that, in MongoDB, a **schema** is just the shape of our data. Unlike SQL databases, we don't set up strict tables with columns at the start, rather the MongoDB allows us to decide, per collection, what fields go in, and we can change or add the new fields later.

The most important thing is to decide: when should we keep related information in the same document, and when should we link documents together by an ID? These are called embedding and referencing.

Embeddings

We now see to an example that we want to store user details and a list of addresses. If the addresses are almost always used with the user (for profile, orders, etc), then we keep them inside the same user document.

Following is the example:

```
{
  "name": "Arjun",
  "email": "arjun@gmail.com",
  "addresses": [
    {"label": "home", "city": "Delhi"},
    {"label": "office", "city": "Bangalore"}
  ]
}
```

This is embedding. It's very fast to fetch and update with one database read or write.

If something might grow big, like thousands of orders per user, it's better to store orders in one collection, users in another, and link them together with a userId.

Following is the example:

```
// user
{
  "_id": "u1",
  "name": "Arjun"
}
// order
{
  "userId": "u1",
  "total": 150,
```

```
  "status": "delivered"
}
```

Now here, we can quickly scan all orders, or all orders for a user.

MongoDB Schema Validation

The MongoDB lets us enforce rules to keep the data clean, even though it's flexible. For example, every **users** document always has an email and phone number:

```
db.createCollection("users", {
  validator: {
    $jsonSchema: {
      bsonType: "object",
      required: ["email", "phone"]
    }
  }
});
```

Here, the insertions that don't match can be blocked.

Keeping Nested Data Simple

Now, I must tell we that MongoDB loves nested data! We can easily have arrays and objects inside documents. We can use this power to keep related things together, like items in an order:

```
{
  "orderId": "o55",
  "userId": "u1",
  "items": [
    {"name": "USB Cable", "qty": 2},
    {"name": "Mouse", "qty": 1}
  ]
}
```

This way, the backend can fetch an order and all its items in a single query.

Query, Update, and Remove

- To find all orders for a user:

```
db.orders.find({userId: "u1"})
```

- To update an address for a user:

```
db.users.updateOne(
  {email: "arjun@gmail.com"},
  {$set: {"addresses.0.city": "Mumbai"}}
)
```

- To remove a single log entry:

```
db.logs.deleteOne({_id: "l22"})
```

It's got embedding, referencing, schema validation and these simple models, so we can design MongoDB for the backend quickly, flexibly and easily, and update it as the project grows.

Performing CRUD Operations

The CRUD stands for Create, Read, Update, Delete, the basic operations every backend needs. In the following, we will get hands-on with the MongoDB syntax for each, and will also look at the results and how to keep things safe with transactions.

Inserting New Records

Let's add a user to our backend:

```
db.users.insertOne({
  name: "Arjun",
  email: "arjun@gmail.com",
  roles: ["user"]
})
```

If successful, MongoDB will reply with something like:

```
{ "acknowledged": true, "insertedId": ObjectId("...") }
```

The **insertedId** is the unique identifier MongoDB generated for the new document.

Fetching Data

Let's find our new user:

```
db.users.findOne({email: "arjun@gmail.com"})
```

This returns the whole user document:

```
{
  "_id": ObjectId("..."),
  "name": "Arjun",
  "email": "arjun@gmail.com",
  "roles": ["user"]
}
```

To get multiple results:

```
db.users.find({roles: "user"})
```

This lists all users with that role.

Changing Existing Records

Say we want to upgrade Arjun to admin:

```
db.users.updateOne(
  {email: "arjun@gmail.com"},
  {$addToSet: {roles: "admin"}}
)
```

Following is the result interpretation:

```
{ "acknowledged": true, "matchedCount": 1, "modifiedCount": 1
}
```

To change his name:

```
db.users.updateOne(
```

```
  {email: "arjun@gmail.com"},
  {$set: {name: "Arjun S."}}
)
```

Removing Data

Suppose we want to remove a user who left:

```
db.users.deleteOne({email: "arjun@gmail.com"})
```

Following is the result interpretation:

```
{ "acknowledged": true, "deletedCount": 1 }
```

Transaction Safety

If we are making the changes, then we want to either **all** succeed or **all** fail. Here, we can use transactions (must be on a replica set):

```
const session = db.getMongo().startSession();
session.startTransaction();
try {
  db.users.updateOne(
    {email: "arjun@gmail.com"},
    {$set: {accountStatus: "closed"}},
    {session}
  );
  db.orders.deleteMany(
    {userId: "u1"},
    {session}
  );
  session.commitTransaction();
} catch (err) {
  session.abortTransaction();
}
```

```
session.endSession();
```

If anything goes wrong, both the actions roll back. Otherwise, both persist.

With all these commands, we can control MongoDB data from the backend project with simple code, instant feedback, and database-managed safety!

Aggregation, Joins, and Indexing

Aggregation

The MongoDB's aggregation framework lets us blend, group, and analyze data on the fly, great for dashboards, analytics, and reporting. Think of aggregation as piping documents through multiple stages (filters, grouping, sorting) to get the exact results we need.

For example, say we want to sum up everyone's order totals by user:

```
db.orders.aggregate([
  { $group: { _id: "$userId", totalSpent: { $sum: "$total" } }
}
])
```

This finds all orders, groups them by **userId**, and adds up their **total**.

You can also add a filter:

```
db.orders.aggregate([
  { $match: { status: "delivered" } },
  { $group: { _id: "$userId", deliveredTotal: { $sum: "$total"
} } }
])
```

Handy for getting stats only for successful orders.

Or, sort and limit for the top spenders:

```
db.orders.aggregate([
  { $group: { _id: "$userId", totalSpent: { $sum: "$total" } }
},
  { $sort: { totalSpent: -1 } },
```

```
  { $limit: 10 }
])
```

Joins

The MongoDB doesn't do SQL-style joins, but starting with v3.2, we get **$lookup**, which lets us "join" two collections.

For instance, if we want to pull user details into orders:

```
db.orders.aggregate([
  {
    $lookup: {
      from: "users",
      localField: "userId",
      foreignField: "_id",
      as: "userInfo"
    }
  }
])
```

From this, each order now has a **userInfo** array containing the matching user.

But, if we only care about the name and email:

```
db.orders.aggregate([
  {
    $lookup: {
      from: "users",
      localField: "userId",
      foreignField: "_id",
      as: "userInfo"
    }
  },
  { $unwind: "$userInfo" },
```

```
  {
    $project: {
      _id: 1,
      total: 1,
      status: 1,
      "userInfo.name": 1,
      "userInfo.email": 1
    }
  }
])
```

We can use **$unwind** to flatten the joined results.

Indexing

The MongoDB can search huge collections quickly thanks to indexes. To make queries speedy, create indexes on fields we filter or sort on.

Say, if we want to add an index on users' email:

```
db.users.createIndex({email: 1}, {unique: true})
```

This makes **find({email: ...})** instant, and ensures no duplicate emails.

And, to speed up order lookups by user and date:

```
db.orders.createIndex({userId: 1, created: -1})
```

Now here, the searches like **db.orders.find({userId: "u1"}).sort({created: -1})** zoom through.

So, to see all indexes (and their fields):

```
db.orders.getIndexes()
```

Optimizing Search and Analysis

Now here, we must not forget to put indexes on fields we query often. If we notice slow queries, then we must use:

```
db.orders.find({userId: "u1"}).explain("executionStats")
```

The MongoDB shows how it searched, if it's using a COLLSCAN (collection scan), add more indexes.

For big analytics, we need to break data up using aggregation, or create summary documents to save dashboard stats ahead of time. We can also use the projection (**`$project`**) so queries return only the fields needed, saving bandwidth and server load.

All these techniques mean the backend project can:

- Group, summarize, and sort data for analytics endpoints.
- Pull in user info for order history with one query.
- Respond fast to user searches and admin reports, even at scale.

With aggregation pipelines, the **`$lookup`** joins, and careful indexing, the MongoDB backend runs smarter, faster, and scales cleanly, no matter how much the dataset grows.

Summary

In this chapter, we learned how databases form the core of backend architecture, supporting persistence, reliability, and transactional integrity for every feature and API. We explored the strengths of MongoDB's flexible document-based data model and how its schema design, through embedding and referencing, can be tailored for user profiles, orders, and log records in our backend projects. We set up MongoDB both locally and in the cloud, detailing secure connection examples and troubleshooting steps to solve authentication and config issues.

We practiced creating, reading, updating, and deleting records, and interpreted the output of each operation along with the use of transactions for operation safety. We implemented complex queries using aggregation pipelines, simulated joins between collections, and built compound indexes for efficient searches and analytics. For tuning and troubleshooting, we used MongoDB's explain feature, server and cloud monitoring dashboards, batch operations, and indexing strategies to detect and resolve slow queries, bottlenecks, and throughput issues. These lessons equipped us to architect, build, and maintain highly reliable, scalable backend systems ready for real-world load and ongoing evolution.

Chapter 6: Crafting REST APIs with gRPC

It's time to think again about backend APIs. This chapter will look at how APIs are the backbone of modern web and cloud platforms. We'll be looking beyond the usual REST stuff, checking out why new protocols like gRPC and GraphQL are becoming so popular, and we'll be comparing these options from the point of view of a backend engineer. We'll get to grips with getting gRPC up and running in a real C++ environment, work through the process of defining service contracts with Protocol Buffers, and see how tidy and well-organised `.proto` files are key to setting up sustainable backend projects.

Moving forward, we'll be designing and setting up a comprehensive CRUD API for a blogging service, adding security with encrypted channels and authentication mechanisms, and improving our application with logging and access controls through interceptors. We'll be doing hands-on debugging, troubleshooting common errors, and adopting best practices for backward-compatible schema evolution. It's all about performance and keeping an eye on our gRPC services, so we can deliver top-notch APIs that meet the needs of today's distributed systems.

APIs beyond REST

API is the name of the game when we're designing web or cloud-native platforms. These aren't just for show; they're the real deal when it comes to keeping the frontend clients, external partners, microservices and data stores in sync. Each time a mobile app syncs a user's data, a web dashboard fetches analytics, or a backend worker processes a transaction, it's the APIs that coordinate the exchange, making sure everything moves smoothly across system boundaries.

So REST has been the go-to for web APIs for a while now, because it's simple to use with HTTP verbs and it uses JSON, which is easy to read. It helps teams get up and running quickly and build services that can be accessed from any environment, whether that's a JavaScript frontend, a Python script, or a mobile app. However, as our systems have grown in size and complexity, we've encountered a few issues.

High-Throughput BottleNecks

The REST APIs operate over **HTTP/1.1** and follow a stateless, request-response pattern. This is perfectly fine for straightforward CRUD operations and low-volume traffic, but it doesn't always keep up with modern expectations. For real-time messaging, live feeds, or backend-to-backend communication at high scale, REST can become a bottleneck:

- Every HTTP connection must be re-established for each request, introducing overhead.
- Multiple endpoints are often required to fetch nested or related data, resulting in over-fetching or under-fetching and making frontends perform extra work to assemble what they need.
- The latency introduced by repeated roundtrips and verbose JSON serialization can add up, especially when millisecond response times are essential.

Type Safety and Schema Drift

Another area where REST starts to show limitations is data typing and contract stability. While tools like Swagger or OpenAPI provide a way to describe RESTful endpoints, the payloads themselves are usually loosely typed JSON. This flexibility is handy, but it opens the door to:

- Type mismatches between client and server
- Silent bugs as APIs evolve, especially across different programming languages
- Security risks from missing or malformed data fields

So here, when APIs form the backbone of distributed, multi-team systems, this lack of strictness becomes a source of technical debt and operational risk.

Modern API Protocols

We, the backend engineers are often tasked with making fundamental decisions about how our systems communicate, both internally and with the outside world. This means choosing the right API protocol for the job. Over the past decade, the REST, gRPC, and GraphQL have become the primary options in this space, each offering a unique set of strengths and trade-offs. While these technologies share a common goal of connecting clients and servers, their design philosophies, data contracts, and performance characteristics differ in meaningful ways that directly impact backend architecture.

REST

The REST quickly became the industry standard for web APIs due to its elegant mapping onto HTTP methods and its human-readable, widely supported data formats (usually JSON). It's easy to get started with REST, spinning up a few endpoints to create, retrieve, update, or delete resources requires only a basic web server and some routing logic.

The REST's strengths are most apparent in loosely coupled environments where interoperability and rapid prototyping matter. Any frontend, be it a browser, mobile app, or even a command-line utility, can send HTTP requests, parse JSON, and interact with a RESTful API with minimal setup. The loosely defined nature of REST payloads (especially with JSON) lets teams iterate quickly, add optional fields, and experiment without being bogged down by strict contracts.

However, the REST's generality can become a liability as systems grow. The lack of enforced typing, combined with the need for multiple round trips to fetch related or nested data, often leads to inefficiencies. The classic REST pattern can struggle to meet the demands of high-performance backends, particularly those requiring strict data validation, low-latency communication, or support for advanced patterns like streaming.

gRPC

The gRPC emerged as a response to the growing complexity and performance requirements of distributed, service-oriented architectures. Instead of relying on HTTP/1.1 and text-based formats, gRPC operates over HTTP/2 and uses Protocol Buffers, a compact, binary serialization format, as its data contract language. Services are described up front in a `.proto` file, which defines messages, fields, and service methods in a way that is both human-readable and machine-enforceable.

Now, what sets gRPC apart for backend engineering is, its focus on interoperability, contract-first development and performance:

- All API interactions are described and validated at compile time, minimizing runtime surprises.
- The Protocol Buffers contract can be used to generate client and server code in dozens of languages, making it easy to build polyglot systems.
- Binary serialization and efficient transport minimize payload sizes and transmission overhead, making gRPC an excellent choice for high-throughput or latency-sensitive workloads.
- Native support for streaming (both server-to-client and client-to-server), bidirectional communication, and built-in support for metadata and authentication.

For backend systems involving many microservices, machine-to-machine communication, or performance-critical paths, the gRPC often becomes the protocol of choice.

GraphQL

The GraphQL addresses a different set of challenges. In many applications, especially those with rich UIs or complex data models, clients either over-fetch (retrieve more data than needed) or under-fetch (require multiple requests to build the required view) using REST endpoints. The GraphQL allows clients to specify exactly which fields and related objects they need, in a single request, via a strongly typed query language.

From a backend perspective, the GraphQL:

- Reduces the number of requests and payload sizes for complex, nested data
- Allows clients to evolve independently by requesting new fields as they become available
- Provides a single endpoint, shifting complexity to the query resolution logic on the backend

However, the GraphQL's flexibility comes with its own considerations. The backend must guard against overly complex queries that could stress the database or expose sensitive fields. Unlike gRPC, GraphQL's runtime typing means that some data contract errors might only surface during execution, not at build time. While GraphQL is less common in machine-to-machine backend integration, it is powerful for client-facing APIs, especially those with fast-changing UIs or composite data views.

Choosing Right Protocol

In our project, we need to connect web clients, mobile apps, and other backend services, each with their own communication requirements.

When to use REST?

If we consider that we need to provide public, easily accessible endpoints for browsing product listings or viewing order history, then REST is the best fit. It has:

- Broad client support (browsers, mobile, partners)
- Simplicity and rapid development
- Minimal setup for authentication, caching, and documentation

A REST endpoint such as **`GET /products`** returning a list of products in JSON is simple for anyone to consume, including external partners.

When to use gRPC?

For backend-to-backend communication, as if, we want the order processor must update the inventory service in real time with minimal latency, then in such case, the gRPC shines. It provides:

- Contract enforcement ensures both services speak the same language
- Fast, binary-encoded payloads
- Native support for streaming updates (e.g., push inventory changes as they happen)

A gRPC call like **`UpdateStock(product_id, quantity)`** can be described in a **`.proto`** file, auto-generating the necessary client and server code.

When to use GraphQL?

If the frontend dashboard needs to build rich, customizable views, pulling not just product data, but also inventory status, user preferences, and promotional banners in one go, then we can opt for GraphQL. It allows:

- frontend to specify exactly which fields it needs
- minimizes the over-fetching and under-fetching
- to adapt gracefully as UI needs evolve

The frontend can send a single query and receive a custom payload tailored for the current view, reducing network overhead and streamlining development.

Protocol Selection

In real backend projects, the decision is rarely either-or. Many robust architectures combine these protocols, selecting the best tool for each job. The REST offers openness and simplicity, gRPC delivers power and efficiency for internal services, and GraphQL empowers client applications with flexible data retrieval.

Requirement/Scenario	REST	gRPC	GraphQL
Public API (external clients)	✓	Possible (less common)	Possible
Internal microservices	Possible	✓	Rare
Language-agnostic integration	✓	✓	✓
Strict data contracts	Limited	✓	Partial
High-throughput/low-latency	Limited	✓	Possible (with tuning)
Streaming/Bidirectional flows	✗	✓	Partial (subscriptions)
Dynamic client-driven data	Limited	✗	✓

From the above, considering who will consume the API, what kind of data flows are needed, and how performance, contract enforcement, and maintainability stack up, we can build backends that are not only technically sound, but also adaptable to future demands.

Getting Started with gRPC

The adoption of gRPC brings a new level of speed, clarity, and cross-language compatibility to our APIs. Before we dive into defining our service contracts and messages, we will get our development environment ready for gRPC. The steps may look technical at first, but by understanding each piece, we set ourselves up for maintainable and powerful backend architecture.

Setting up gRPC and Protocol Buffers

Most of the modern backend systems run on Linux, and hence the gRPC's tooling is designed to feel at home there. Following is how we proceed further:

Install Protocol Buffers Compiler

The Protocol Buffers, or Protobuf, are the backbone of gRPC contracts. We use **`protoc`** to generate C++ classes from our service and message definitions. So here, we download the latest release from the official Protocol Buffers GitHub. After this, we extract the archive and move into the directory.

In the directory, we build and install:

```
./configure

make

sudo make install
```

Clone and Build gRPC

The gRPC source contains everything required, including C++ plugins for code generation. Here, we then clone the gRPC repository:

```
git clone -b $(curl -L https://grpc.io/release)
https://github.com/grpc/grpc

cd grpc

git submodule update --init

make

sudo make install
```

After this, we then build the C++ plugin for gRPC:

```
make grpc_cpp_plugin

sudo make install-grpc_cpp_plugin
```

Link Dependencies

When starting a new Backend project, make sure to link the required gRPC and protobuf libraries in the **`CMakeLists.txt`** or build system. You'll typically include **`grpc++`**, **`protobuf`**, and their respective header paths.

Structuring a .proto file

We know that our backend provides blogging service. Now, we want clients to be able to add new posts, fetch posts, update them, and delete them. So here, we write a **.proto** file that describes all the required messages and service methods, as shown below:

```
syntax = "proto3";
package blog;
// The blog post message type.
message Post {
  string id = 1;
  string title = 2;
  string author = 3;
  string content = 4;
}
// The response message containing the blog post ID.
message PostResponse {
  string id = 1;
}
// The response message containing a full blog post.
message FullPostResponse {
  Post post = 1;
}
// The Blog service definition.
service BlogService {
  // Sends a new blog post.
  rpc AddPost(Post) returns (PostResponse);
  // Retrieves a blog post.
  rpc GetPost(PostResponse) returns (FullPostResponse);
  // Updates a blog post.
  rpc UpdatePost(Post) returns (PostResponse);
  // Deletes a blog post.
```

```
  rpc DeletePost(PostResponse) returns (PostResponse);
}
```

In the above file,

- The **syntax = "proto3"** sets the version. It ensures access to the latest language features and conventions.
- The **package blog** namespaces the definitions to avoid collisions in larger systems.
- Each **message** describes the payload for an RPC method. The field numbers (**= 1;**, **= 2;**, etc.) are required and enable versioning and backward compatibility.
- The **service** block collects all related RPCs under a single interface. It let us generate idiomatic server and client code for any supported language.

Generating C++ Code from .proto

With our **.proto** contract defined, we then use the **protoc** compiler to generate C++ source files. These files handle all the serialization, deserialization, and service plumbing for us.

```
protoc --proto_path=. --grpc_out=. --plugin=protoc-gen-
grpc=`which grpc_cpp_plugin` blog_service.proto
```

This command outputs **.pb.h** and **.pb.cc** files for messages, plus service stubs for our backend.

This whole process delivers strict typing, code generation, and the ability to evolve our APIs confidently, no matter how complex the requirements become. In the next steps, we'll bring these contracts to life by generating server and client code, wiring up handlers, and implementing real backend logic.

Building CRUD gRPC API

We're going to build a simple yet scalable blogging backend using gRPC and C++. We will design the API contract, implement the backend handlers, and wire everything up for Create, Read, Update, and Delete operations. It will show us a cleanly defined **.proto** contract getting transformed into a robust server logic, and we can then use it as a strong template for our future backend CRUD projects.

Defining API Contract

The first thing we do is outline exactly what operations our service will perform and what data shapes it will exchange. So, in our blogging backend, the API needs to allow users to add a post, fetch a single post, update existing content, delete a post, and list all posts. Each of the operation becomes a remote procedure call (RPC), and each request or response is a typed message.

In the following, we will see how the API contract is captured in our **`blog_service.proto`** file:

```
syntax = "proto3";
package blog;
// Represents a blog post
message Post {
  string id = 1;
  string title = 2;
  string author = 3;
  string content = 4;
}
// Message for sending just the ID
message PostId {
  string id = 1;
}
// Wraps a single post for responses
message PostResponse {
  Post post = 1;
}
// Returns multiple posts
message PostsResponse {
  repeated Post posts = 1;
}
// Main blog service interface
service BlogService {
  rpc CreatePost(Post) returns (PostId);
  rpc GetPost(PostId) returns (PostResponse);
```

```
  rpc UpdatePost(Post) returns (PostId);
  rpc DeletePost(PostId) returns (PostId);
  rpc ListPosts(google.protobuf.Empty) returns
(PostsResponse);
}
```

This contract is precise. In it, every field is typed, each RPC method has a clear input and output, and listing all posts is handled in a scalable way with the **`repeated`** field.

Generating Backend Code

Now that our API contract is written, we then proceed to code generation. The Protocol Buffers compiler, **`protoc`**, takes this **`.proto`** file and produces C++ classes for all messages and the BlogService interface. These files handle the work of serialization, deserialization, and basic service plumbing, freeing us to focus on the business logic.

So, now to generate the code:

```
protoc --proto_path=. --grpc_out=. --plugin=protoc-gen-
grpc=`which grpc_cpp_plugin` blog_service.proto
```

The generated code will provide base classes and stubs we will extend to create the server.

Implementing Server Handlers

The actual or the real hands-on part begins now as the code is generated. So here, we set up a **`BlogServiceImpl`** class, which inherits from the generated service interface. To keep things practical and easy to follow, we will use an in-memory C++ map to store blog posts and a mutex for thread safety.

So, in a production backend, we will replace this with persistent storage, but the structure remains very similar as shown below:

```
#include "blog_service.grpc.pb.h"
#include <grpcpp/grpcpp.h>
#include <unordered_map>
#include <mutex>
#include <string>
class BlogServiceImpl final : public
blog::BlogService::Service {
```

```
public:
  // In-memory post store
  std::unordered_map<std::string, blog::Post> posts_;
  std::mutex data_mutex_;
  // Generates unique IDs (for demo, use timestamp or counter)
  std::string GenerateId() {
    static int counter = 1;
    return "post_" + std::to_string(counter++);
  }
  // Handler for Create
  grpc::Status CreatePost(grpc::ServerContext* context, const
blog::Post* request,
                          blog::PostId* response) override {
    std::lock_guard<std::mutex> lock(data_mutex_);
    std::string id = GenerateId();
    blog::Post post = *request;
    post.set_id(id);
    posts_[id] = post;
    response->set_id(id);
    return grpc::Status::OK;
  }
  // Handler for Read
  grpc::Status GetPost(grpc::ServerContext* context, const
blog::PostId* request,
                       blog::PostResponse* response) override
{
    std::lock_guard<std::mutex> lock(data_mutex_);
    auto it = posts_.find(request->id());
    if (it == posts_.end()) {
```

```
      return grpc::Status(grpc::StatusCode::NOT_FOUND, "Post
not found");
    }
    *(response->mutable_post()) = it->second;
    return grpc::Status::OK;
  }
  // Handler for Update
  grpc::Status UpdatePost(grpc::ServerContext* context, const
blog::Post* request,
                          blog::PostId* response) override {
    std::lock_guard<std::mutex> lock(data_mutex_);
    auto it = posts_.find(request->id());
    if (it == posts_.end()) {
      return grpc::Status(grpc::StatusCode::NOT_FOUND, "Post
not found");
    }
    posts_[request->id()] = *request;
    response->set_id(request->id());
    return grpc::Status::OK;
  }
  // Handler for Delete
  grpc::Status DeletePost(grpc::ServerContext* context, const
blog::PostId* request,
                          blog::PostId* response) override {
    std::lock_guard<std::mutex> lock(data_mutex_);
    if (posts_.erase(request->id()) == 0) {
      return grpc::Status(grpc::StatusCode::NOT_FOUND, "Post
not found");
    }
    response->set_id(request->id());
    return grpc::Status::OK;
```

```
  }
  // Handler for List
  grpc::Status ListPosts(grpc::ServerContext* context, const
google::protobuf::Empty* request,
                         blog::PostsResponse* response)
override {
    std::lock_guard<std::mutex> lock(data_mutex_);
    for (const auto& pair : posts_) {
      *response->add_posts() = pair.second;
    }
    return grpc::Status::OK;
  }
};
```

Bringing CRUD API to Life

Now that the handlers are written, the service is ready to register with a gRPC server and begin accepting real requests. Each method receives typed C++ objects, performs thread-safe operations, and responds according to the contract we laid out in the **`.proto`** file.

This is how a cleanly defined gRPC contract, combined with thoughtful C++ implementation, yields a backend API that is predictable, maintainable, and ready to scale.

Hardening gRPC APIs

Every robust backend has to ensure that sensitive data is kept private, access is strictly controlled, and every interaction is monitored for integrity and policy compliance. The gRPC is built with these priorities in mind. It offers built-in tools for secure communication, authentication, and operational controls.

Creating Secure Channels

The TLS serves as the foundation for safe communication in distributed systems. When we transmit information such as user credentials, payment details, or confidential business data, transmitting it in plain text is simply not an option. The TLS encrypts each byte that moves across the network. It makes unreadable to unintended recipients and protecting the data from interception or manipulation.

So, all we need to do to set up TLS with gRPC is prepare a certificate and a private key, which are usually provided as **.crt** and **.key** files. We can get these from a Certificate Authority or make them yourself for development and internal services. When it's ready, the backend will load these files and set up the gRPC server to only accept encrypted connections. This means that every API call is protected by the kind of encryption that the industry uses as a standard.

Up next, in the server code, we start by reading the certificate and key files, and then we set up the SSL credentials for our server. The gRPC server builder then uses these credentials, and any clients connecting will need to trust the server's certificate to establish the channel.

```
#include <grpcpp/security/server_credentials.h>
std::string server_cert = ReadFile("server.crt");
std::string server_key = ReadFile("server.key");
grpc::SslServerCredentialsOptions::PemKeyCertPair key_cert =
{server_key, server_cert};
grpc::SslServerCredentialsOptions ssl_opts;
ssl_opts.pem_key_cert_pairs.push_back(key_cert);
auto server_creds = grpc::SslServerCredentials(ssl_opts);
std::unique_ptr<grpc::Server> server = grpc::ServerBuilder()
    .AddListeningPort(server_address, server_creds)
    .RegisterService(&service_impl)
    .BuildAndStart();
```

This setup means every connection to our backend is encrypted from end to end, with no need for manual data handling or additional encryption routines in the application code.

API Authentication with Metadata and Tokens

While TLS secures the transport layer, it remains essential to control access at the application level as well. Not every client or user should have equal permissions. With gRPC, the solution revolves around **metadata**, which functions as a flexible set of headers that travel with each request. This metadata is the ideal place to send authentication information such as API keys, session tokens, or JWTs.

Within a C++ backend, we check the metadata from the request context for an authorization token. If a valid token is present and passes verification, the handler proceeds with its logic. Otherwise, the handler returns an unauthenticated status, effectively denying access.

```
grpc::Status BlogServiceImpl::CreatePost(grpc::ServerContext*
context,
                                          const blog::Post*
request,
                                          blog::PostId*
response) {
  const auto& client_metadata = context->client_metadata();
  auto it = client_metadata.find("authorization");
  if (it == client_metadata.end() || !IsValidToken(it-
>second.data(), it->second.length())) {
    return grpc::Status(grpc::StatusCode::UNAUTHENTICATED,
"Missing or invalid token");
  }
  // Business logic proceeds here
}
```

The clients attach metadata by setting the appropriate header in the context. In collaborative backend development, this approach allows us to enforce permissions, implement API rate tiers, or integrate with external authentication systems such as OAuth2 or identity providers.

Adding Interceptors

The **Interceptors** in gRPC helps to insert custom logic before or after API calls. An interceptor in C++ inherits from **`grpc::experimental::ServerInterceptor`** and acts on each incoming call. With interceptors, it becomes straightforward to log requests, maintain audit trails, or enforce rate limits across services.

For instance, a logging interceptor can record method names and timestamps, helping with monitoring or debugging. The rate limiting logic can count requests per client and return a throttling status if limits are exceeded.

Following is the sample program:

```
class LoggingInterceptor : public
grpc::experimental::ServerInterceptor {
 public:
  void Intercept(grpc::experimental::ServerInterceptorInfo*
info) override {
```

```
        std::string method = info->method();
        std::cout << "API call: " << method << std::endl;
        info->Proceed();
    }
};
```

When building the server, we register our interceptors so that every API call is automatically processed through these checks. This pattern keeps the business logic clean and maintainable while providing a centralized place to enforce policy.

Troubleshooting gRPC Services

There's more to being a software developer than just writing service logic. If we want to be a successful developer, we need to test a lot, solve real-world problems and always think about how to deal with any tiny integration issues. If we walk through a scenario where we encounter and troubleshoot real issues, we'll develop the habits needed to keep our APIs robust and production-ready.

Incompatible Proto files

Our blogging backend is so far deployed in two environments; a staging server running the latest proto contract, and a client still using an outdated version. If there is a new field, **`timestamp`**, has been added to the **`Post`** message in the proto file, but the client has not regenerated its code. When we run the client and attempt to create or fetch posts, the error appear.

So here, the observed problem is:

- The client receives an error, such as **`INTERNAL: Failed to parse server response`**.
- The server logs indicate deserialization problems or missing required fields.

Inspecting Payloads and Contracts

We start troubleshooting by confirming both the client and the server are using the same proto contract. On both ends, we add code to log the incoming and outgoing payloads using the **`DebugString()`** method available on protobuf messages.

```
// On the server, inside the handler:
std::cout << "Received request: " << request.DebugString() <<
std::endl;
```

If the client is sending a **Post** message without the new **timestamp** field, the server's logs will reveal its absence. Similarly, logging the response at the client side can help verify if fields are missing or incorrectly formatted.

Regenerating and Synchronizing Proto files

Upon confirming the mismatch, we ensure both the server and client use the latest **.proto** file. On both systems, we re-run the Protocol Buffers compiler:

```
protoc --proto_path=. --grpc_out=. --plugin=protoc-gen-
grpc=`which grpc_cpp_plugin` blog_service.proto
```

We rebuild both applications. This step often resolves serialization errors due to contract drift. After redeployment, we observe that the client now receives valid responses, with the expected fields present.

Analyzing gRPC Status and Error Codes

Sometimes, even after updating, the client receives a **NOT_FOUND** error when fetching a post. This status tells us the issue is in the business logic rather than serialization. We check the server handler for **GetPost** and confirm it returns this status when the requested ID is absent from the data store.

```
if (posts_.find(request->id()) == posts_.end()) {
  return grpc::Status(grpc::StatusCode::NOT_FOUND, "Post not
found");
}
```

From here, we might test again, and able to check if the client is passing a valid post ID. The logging of the request on both ends helps verify the exact value sent and received.

Debugging with Network and Channel Tools

Suppose a client still reports **UNAVAILABLE: failed to connect to all addresses**. This points to a network or server configuration issue. We check:

- Is the server running and listening on the correct port?
- Are there any firewall rules or network issues blocking the connection?

We then use tools like **netstat**, **lsof**, or gRPC's own verbose channel tracing (enabled by setting **GRPC_VERBOSITY=DEBUG** and **GRPC_TRACE=all** as environment variables) to inspect whether the connection attempts reach the backend. This low-level inspection confirms whether the problem is in our code or in the network setup.

Backward Compatibility and Schema Evolution

To practice backward-compatible evolution, so here we add new optional fields to messages and always use new field numbers. Removing or reusing field numbers is avoided. For example, if we add an **`editor`** field to **`Post`**, we ensure existing clients, unaware of the new field, continue to work as before, since protobuf simply ignores unknown fields. In automated tests, we use both the old and new clients against the updated server to verify nothing breaks.

Through this hands-on process, logging message contents, synchronizing contracts, interpreting error codes, inspecting network connections, and maintaining careful schema evolution, we transform troubleshooting from guesswork into a set of reliable steps.

gRPC Performance Tuning

There's a lot more to delivering a high-performance backend than just picking an efficient protocol. After our gRPC APIs are up and running, we've got to keep an eye on how they behave under real workloads, how they scale with demand, and how quickly they respond to client requests. The best way to do this is to work out what the real bottlenecks are, adjust the payloads and make the most of C++ concurrency features. Basically, we keep an eye on how things are performing, which gives us the info we need to make improvements.

Diagnosing Slow Calls

There will be times when our blogging backend may experience periodic slowdowns, perhaps some requests are taking several hundred milliseconds instead of a few. So here, the first step is to identify which parts of the stack are responsible.

To do this, we introduce structured logging with precise timestamps at every major stage of request processing. For this, within our service handler, we measure how long each step takes by capturing time points before and after database access, business logic execution, or outbound calls as shown below:

```
#include <chrono>
#include <iostream>
grpc::Status BlogServiceImpl::GetPost(grpc::ServerContext*
context,
                                      const blog::PostId*
request,
                                      blog::PostResponse*
response) {
  auto start = std::chrono::steady_clock::now();
```

```
  // Simulate data fetch
  auto it = posts_.find(request->id());
  if (it == posts_.end()) {
    return grpc::Status(grpc::StatusCode::NOT_FOUND, "Post not
found");
  }
  *(response->mutable_post()) = it->second;
  auto end = std::chrono::steady_clock::now();
  auto duration =
std::chrono::duration_cast<std::chrono::milliseconds>(end -
start).count();
  std::cout << "GetPost processing time: " << duration << "
ms" << std::endl;
  return grpc::Status::OK;
}
```

If we discover the bottleneck is inside our business logic or data store, then we can profile that segment further. If processing is consistently fast but the end-to-end call is slow, network latency or payload size may be the cause.

Optimizing Payloads

The large verbose messages can have a major impact on both latency and throughput. Now, to optimize, we need to examine the size and content of our payloads. For this, the Protocol Buffers API allows us to check the serialized size before sending data as shown below:

```
size_t payload_size = response->ByteSizeLong();
std::cout << "Response payload size: " << payload_size << "
bytes" << std::endl;
```

In the above, if the payloads are large, we look for opportunities to trim unnecessary fields, replace repeated or nested data with references or summaries, and avoid over-fetching in the service logic. For example, if our **ListPosts** method returns every field for every post but clients only need titles and IDs, we introduce a lighter response message:

```
message PostSummary {
  string id = 1;
```

```
  string title = 2;
}
message PostsSummaryResponse {
  repeated PostSummary posts = 1;
}
service BlogService {
  rpc ListPostSummaries(google.protobuf.Empty) returns
(PostsSummaryResponse);
}
```

In the above, by sending only what clients need, we are able to reduce the bandwidth and serialization overhead. This directly translates to faster calls.

Concurrency and Thread-Pool Tuning

The gRPC servers in C++ can handle lots of requests at once by using thread pools. It'll balance requests across available CPU cores by default, but to get the best performance, we will need to tweak this to match the specific workload.

We can set the number of threads to use for request handling when building the server. This is set with the **SetSyncServerOption** method on the **ServerBuilder**:

```
grpc::ServerBuilder builder;
builder.AddListeningPort(server_address,
grpc::InsecureServerCredentials());
builder.RegisterService(&service_impl);
// For example, set the thread pool to 8 threads
builder.SetSyncServerOption(grpc::ServerBuilder::SyncServerOpt
ion::NUM_CQS, 4);
builder.SetSyncServerOption(grpc::ServerBuilder::SyncServerOpt
ion::MIN_POLLERS, 8);
builder.SetSyncServerOption(grpc::ServerBuilder::SyncServerOpt
ion::MAX_POLLERS, 16);
std::unique_ptr<grpc::Server> server(builder.BuildAndStart());
```

In the above, by testing with different values, we can monitor the average and peak response times under concurrent loads. If increasing thread count improves throughput and reduces queueing time, our backend was CPU bound; if not, we may be limited by external resources (such as database I/O) and should optimize there.

Summary

Throughout this chapter, we took a look at how APIs became the basis of backend communication, and how traditional REST approaches sometimes didn't meet the needs of modern, high-throughput, or strongly typed distributed systems. We compared REST, gRPC and GraphQL, and learned a lot about when each one worked best in real backend projects. We got hands-on and installed and configured gRPC in a C++ backend, defined robust service contracts with Protocol Buffers, and learned to organise .proto files for long-term maintainability. We got to see the whole process of setting up a CRUD blogging service, and how contract definitions are turned into efficient server handlers.

We made our backend stronger with TLS-secured channels, added authentication with metadata and tokens, and extended our codebase with interceptors for logging and operational control. We looked at practical scenarios, like fixing problems with the protocol and checking live payloads, and our approach to backward compatibility was all about safe, step-by-step changes. At last, we made some performance tweaks by spotting slow requests, tweaking message payloads and balancing concurrency through thread-pool configuration.

Chapter 7: Dealing with Client-Side and Server-Side Caching

We're going to take a close look at how caching works for Backend development, and how it can make the systems faster and more reliable. So, first we'll get to grips with the main principles of caching, and see how it links up the fast application logic with the slower data sources. As we go through the modules, we'll learn to set up practical caching layers, using both in-memory maps and powerful tools like Redis to speed up data retrieval in real backend scenarios.

The chapter will walk us through the essential eviction strategies, like LRU, LFU and RR, showing us not only how they work, but also how to bring them to life with C++ code that's tailored for different usage patterns. We'll take on the real-world challenge of cache consistency, mastering techniques for invalidation, freshness, and synchronization, even in distributed and multi-node environments. By the time we're done, we will have the hands-on troubleshooting skills to figure out how to boost cache performance, spot common problems like stale data or stampede, and build monitoring solutions to keep things running smoothly as traffic and data grow.

Fundamentals of Caching in C++ Backends

The concept of caching remains one of the foundational tools for delivering high-performance in backend architectures. With applications grow to serve millions of users, the factors of speed and responsiveness become the defining benchmarks of success. Within this landscape, the caching acts as the mechanism that bridges the gap between the rapid-fire demands of client requests and the comparatively slower world of persistent storage, external APIs, or complex computation. In C++ backends, every millisecond saved by a cache hit reduces user-perceived latency, keeps servers responsive during peak traffic, and preserves database and network resources for the most critical operations.

So here, a well-placed cache transforms the system's ability to handle repeated requests for popular or expensive-to-generate data. For a user-facing application, this might mean that the most-read blog posts, most-frequent analytics, or even session tokens are always instantly available, while for backend services, it could mean that API responses, expensive aggregations, or authentication tokens are served from memory instead of being recalculated or retrieved every time. The effect is twofold, which is that the user experience improves as response times drop, and the other is that the backend infrastructure gains resilience and scalability by offloading work from its most stressed components.

Server-Side Caching

When we use server-side caching, it creates an intermediary storage layer that sits between clients and the main backend resources. Basically, this means the backend application itself, or a dedicated caching layer, temporarily holds the results of frequent or expensive operations. This could be things like HTML pages, the output of an API, or even objects from an external service. In short, if we have already done the work, and we are likely to need it again soon, the cache will save it for you, so we don't have to repeat the same work. This reduces server load, accelerates response times, and handles sudden bursts of traffic like a pro.

In-Memory Caching

The idea behind in-memory caching is to use the speed of RAM to keep the most useful data close to the application logic. When data is read a lot more often than it's updated, like with user profiles, permissions or static configuration, in-memory caches are really useful. This data is in memory, so accessing it is much quicker than having to go to a disk or an external service. In C++, we can use STL containers for simple use cases or high-performance external solutions like Redis or Memcached for larger, distributed systems. You'll find this approach really useful for applications where even a small delay can have a big impact on the user experience, especially if that application is latency-sensitive.

Database Caching

The database is often the slowest part of a modern backend system, especially when handling complex queries or operating at scale. And so here, the database caching addresses this bottleneck by intercepting repeated queries and storing their results for quick reuse. Instead of recalculating the same aggregation or retrieving the same records on each request, the backend first checks the cache and only reaches out to the database if the answer is not already available. There are popular open-source tools such as Redis that can be seamlessly integrated with C++ applications to serve as robust database caches, providing time-to-live controls, eviction policies, and persistence options.

So, if all the caches are correctly layered and tuned, the backend can serve frequent data with microsecond latency, dramatically reducing the time users wait for responses. This rapid turnaround allows the application to sustain far higher levels of concurrent traffic, prevents slowdowns under load, and reduces operational costs by keeping expensive database or computation resources free for the cases that truly require them.

Implementing Caching Layers

Building In-Memory Caching

In our project, we want to serve blog post content quickly and reduce database load. We start by setting up an in-memory cache using a standard C++ map, where the key is the blog post ID and the value is the post content or object. When a request arrives to fetch a blog post, the logic first checks if the requested post is available in the in-memory cache. If it is, the cache returns the result immediately, no database lookup or expensive computation required. If the post is not present in the cache, the service queries the database, retrieves the result, and stores it in the cache for future access.

For updates, after a post is edited or replaced in the database, the cache entry is refreshed with the new value. This approach, known as the **cache-aside strategy**, puts the cache "beside" the database, and the application explicitly manages both sources of truth. The process keeps the cache simple and predictable while avoiding the risk of serving stale data.

Following is a quick practical implementation of it:

```
#include <unordered_map>
#include <mutex>
#include <string>
class BlogCache {
public:
    // Simulated in-memory cache
    std::unordered_map<std::string, std::string> cache;
    std::mutex cache_mutex;
    // Fetch from cache or load from database
    std::string GetPost(const std::string& post_id) {
        std::lock_guard<std::mutex> lock(cache_mutex);
        auto it = cache.find(post_id);
        if (it != cache.end()) {
            return it->second; // Cache hit
        }
        std::string post = LoadPostFromDatabase(post_id); //
Simulate DB fetch
        cache[post_id] = post;
        return post;
    }
    // Update both cache and database
    void UpdatePost(const std::string& post_id, const
std::string& content) {
        UpdatePostInDatabase(post_id, content);
        std::lock_guard<std::mutex> lock(cache_mutex);
        cache[post_id] = content; // Cache refresh after DB
update
```

```
    }
    // Simulated functions for the demo
    std::string LoadPostFromDatabase(const std::string&
post_id) { /* ... */ }
    void UpdatePostInDatabase(const std::string& post_id,
const std::string& content) { /* ... */ }
};
```

This method allows us to take control of caching logic within the backend. It ensures every post fetch is as fast as possible while every update remains consistent.

Integrating Redis for Distributed Database Caching

Once our backend becomes distributed across multiple processes or machines, the in-memory caching no longer scales. So here, an external cache engine like **Redis** can contribute. It is an open-source, in-memory key-value store designed for low latency and high throughput. To me, it is a perfect candidate for database caching in backend services.

So now, to use Redis in our backend, we will use a client library such as hiredis or redis-plus-plus. The **cache-aside** strategy still applies. It is a strategy where the application code explicitly manages the cache and database, pulling data into the cache as needed and pushing updates after writes. This method gives us control but requires discipline to avoid stale data. when fetching a blog post, we check Redis first. If the cache does not have the post, the backend queries the database, stores the result in Redis, and returns it.

Following is a simplified integration of our project with Redis:

```
#include <sw/redis++/redis++.h>
using namespace sw::redis;
Redis redis("tcp://127.0.0.1:6379");
// Cache-aside for fetch
std::string GetPost(const std::string& post_id) {
    auto cached = redis.get(post_id);
    if (cached) {
        return *cached; // Redis cache hit
    }
    std::string post = LoadPostFromDatabase(post_id); //
Simulate DB fetch
```

```
    redis.set(post_id, post); // Cache in Redis
    return post;
}
// Write-through for update
void UpdatePost(const std::string& post_id, const std::string&
content) {
    UpdatePostInDatabase(post_id, content);
    redis.set(post_id, content); // Refresh cache in Redis
}
```

In this model, the Redis becomes a shared, fast-access cache across all backend instances. The code ensures that all reads and writes stay consistent between the database and cache.

Cache Eviction Strategies

Every cache, no matter how large, has a finite capacity. After the cache fills up, we need to decide which items to remove to make room for fresher content. And, this process is called eviction, and the strategy chosen directly affects both the hit rate and the overall performance of a backend system.

Now here, choosing the right eviction policy depends on the patterns of data access, the nature of the workload, and how predictable the popularity of cached items is over time. We will see to them in the below subtopics.

Least Recently Used (LRU)

The **LRU** policy removes the entry that has not been accessed for the longest period. This works well when recent data is likely to be requested again soon, such as trending blog posts or active user sessions.

To implement an LRU cache in C++, a combination of a hash map and a doubly linked list is commonly used. Each time an item is accessed or updated, it is moved to the front of the list. When eviction is needed, the item at the back of the list, the least recently used one, is removed.

Following is a simplified LRU cache for our blog posts:

```
#include <unordered_map>
#include <list>
#include <string>
```

```
class LRUCache {
public:
    LRUCache(size_t capacity) : capacity_(capacity) {}
    std::string Get(const std::string& post_id) {
        auto it = cache_.find(post_id);
        if (it == cache_.end()) return ""; // Cache miss
        order_.splice(order_.begin(), order_, it->second.second); // Move accessed node to front
        return it->second.first;
    }
    void Put(const std::string& post_id, const std::string& content) {
        auto it = cache_.find(post_id);
        if (it != cache_.end()) {
            order_.splice(order_.begin(), order_, it->second.second);
            it->second.first = content;
            return;
        }
        if (cache_.size() == capacity_) {
            std::string old = order_.back();
            order_.pop_back();
            cache_.erase(old);
        }
        order_.push_front(post_id);
        cache_[post_id] = {content, order_.begin()};
    }
private:
    size_t capacity_;
    std::list<std::string> order_;
```

```
    std::unordered_map<std::string, std::pair<std::string,
std::list<std::string>::iterator>> cache_;
};
```

This design ensures recent accesses keep the relevant data available. It is ideal for workloads with strong temporal locality.

Least Frequently Used (LFU)

It's all about highlighting the entries that nobody's ever used. When certain data is always popular, like always-requested metadata or evergreen content, the **LFU** helps make the cache as useful as possible.

An LFU cache keeps track of how often each item is used. When the cache is full, the entry with the lowest count is removed. So, to get LFU working efficiently, we need to use maps to store counts and keep lists or sets of items for each frequency.

A basic LFU cache for blog posts might look like as below:

```
#include <unordered_map>
#include <set>
#include <string>
class LFUCache {
public:
    LFUCache(size_t capacity) : capacity_(capacity) {}
    std::string Get(const std::string& post_id) {
        if (cache_.find(post_id) == cache_.end()) return "";
        freq_[post_id]++;
        return cache_[post_id];
    }
    void Put(const std::string& post_id, const std::string&
content) {
        if (cache_.size() == capacity_ && cache_.find(post_id)
== cache_.end()) {
            std::string lfu;
            int min_freq = INT_MAX;
```

```
            for (const auto& pair : freq_) {
                if (pair.second < min_freq) {
                    min_freq = pair.second;
                    lfu = pair.first;
                }
            }
            cache_.erase(lfu);
            freq_.erase(lfu);
        }
        cache_[post_id] = content;
        freq_[post_id]++;
    }
private:
    size_t capacity_;
    std::unordered_map<std::string, std::string> cache_;
    std::unordered_map<std::string, int> freq_;
};
```

Although simple, this pattern efficiently retains content with lasting popularity, making it suitable for caches where some items are accessed far more often than others.

Random Replacement (RR)

The **RR** provides a straightforward alternative. So, when eviction is needed, the cache randomly selects an entry to remove. This policy is easy to implement and can perform surprisingly well when access patterns are unpredictable or uniformly distributed.

Given below is the setup of RR for our blog post cache:

```
#include <unordered_map>
#include <vector>
#include <string>
#include <cstdlib>
class RRCache {
```

```
public:
    RRCache(size_t capacity) : capacity_(capacity) {}
    std::string Get(const std::string& post_id) {
        if (cache_.find(post_id) == cache_.end()) return "";
        return cache_[post_id];
    }
    void Put(const std::string& post_id, const std::string&
content) {
        if (cache_.size() == capacity_ && cache_.find(post_id)
== cache_.end()) {
            int idx = rand() % keys_.size();
            cache_.erase(keys_[idx]);
            keys_.erase(keys_.begin() + idx);
        }
        cache_[post_id] = content;
        keys_.push_back(post_id);
    }
private:
    size_t capacity_;
    std::unordered_map<std::string, std::string> cache_;
    std::vector<std::string> keys_;
};
```

The backend of RR sidesteps the overhead of tracking usage or frequency, making it lightweight and effective for certain general-purpose caches.

The best method depends on the real access patterns. The LRU model works best when recent access is a good indicator of future use, like in active session management. But LFU really shines when some content stays popular over time, like in recommendation engines. And if we are dealing with unpredictable or uniform workloads, RR's got us covered. The key is to understand and practise each approach, and that is how we can be sure that our cache always serves the right data, boosts performance and supports scalability under a variety of backend demands.

Cache Consistency and Handling Invalidation

In backend caching, one of the persistent challenges is making sure the data in our cache always reflects the latest state of the underlying database or service. If a cache returns outdated or "stale" data, users experience inconsistencies, and business logic may operate on incorrect information. To maintain confidence in cached results, it is essential to adopt robust strategies for cache consistency and timely invalidation.

Maintaining Cache Data Fresh

Every time a post is updated or deleted in the database, the cache needs to reflect that change without delay. Otherwise, the users might see old versions or even data that no longer exists.

If we want to take a more practical approach, we could start by tying cache updates or invalidations directly to database write operations. So, when we update a blog post, the backend either overwrites the cache entry with the new content or removes the entry completely. This means that the next read has to fetch from the database. This makes sure that anyone who comes after we always gets fresh data.

```
void UpdateBlogPost(const std::string& post_id, const
std::string& new_content) {
    UpdatePostInDatabase(post_id, new_content); // Update DB
first
    std::lock_guard<std::mutex> lock(cache_mutex);
    cache[post_id] = new_content; // Update or refresh cache
}
void DeleteBlogPost(const std::string& post_id) {
    DeletePostFromDatabase(post_id);
    std::lock_guard<std::mutex> lock(cache_mutex);
    cache.erase(post_id); // Remove from cache after DB delete
}
```

This approach is called as **write-through** or **write-back**. It keeps the cache and database remain synchronized in response to every change.

Cache Invalidation Techniques

There are several ways to automatically keep cached data from becoming outdated:

Time-to-Live (TTL)

The idea is to set an expiry time on cache entries so that after a fixed duration, they're automatically invalidated and removed. When the next request comes in, the backend gets the latest value from the source and fills the cache again. A lot of cache libraries, including Redis, support TTL natively.

Explicit Invalidation

On any write operation, such as create, update, or delete, the backend explicitly deletes or refreshes the affected cache entry. This is reliable and avoids serving stale data but requires careful coordination between the cache and database operations.

Versioning and Timestamps

If we include a version number or last-modified timestamp in the cache key or as part of the value, that would be great. Every time there's a request, the backend checks if the cached version matches the current state in the database. If they don't match, the cache is updated or invalidated.

Each of these above techniques helps maintain cache freshness, though the right choice depends on how often the data changes and how critical real-time consistency is for the application.

Handling Cache Stampede

A cache stampede occurs when a popular cache entry expires or is invalidated, and multiple concurrent requests simultaneously try to fetch the missing data from the backend source. This can overwhelm the system, especially if the computation or query is expensive.

So here, a practical mitigation is the **lock or single-flight pattern**. When a cache miss happens, the first request takes responsibility for fetching and repopulating the cache, while subsequent requests wait for the new value to appear.

You may witness in the following sample program:

```
std::string GetBlogPost(const std::string& post_id) {
    {
        std::lock_guard<std::mutex> lock(cache_mutex);
        auto it = cache.find(post_id);
        if (it != cache.end()) return it->second;
    }
    std::unique_lock<std::mutex> lock(fetch_mutex); // Ensure
only one fetch
    std::string post = LoadPostFromDatabase(post_id);
```

```
    {
        std::lock_guard<std::mutex> cache_lock(cache_mutex);
        cache[post_id] = post;
    }
    return post;
}
```

In the above, the structure prevents a surge of duplicate database queries, especially under heavy load or for frequently accessed content.

Synchronizing Cache

If a bunch of backend instances share a cache, consistency becomes a distributed problem. All instances need to agree on when to invalidate or refresh entries. If we use TTL, explicit cache invalidation on every write, and atomic operations offered by external caches like Redis, we can make sure all nodes see consistent, up-to-date data. In some setups, message queues or pub/sub notifications are used to broadcast cache invalidation events to every backend instance, so caches across the fleet stay in sync after any data change.

When we actively manage cache invalidation, prevent stampede conditions, and synchronise cache state across all backend processes, we make sure that the cache provides not just speed, but also accuracy and reliability. These patterns help every Backend project deliver the right results, no matter what changes happen with data, users, and infrastructure.

Troubleshooting Cache Performance

The production-grade projects reveal various issues such as stale data, cache stampedes, or node inconsistencies. And resolving these issues quickly is very much essential for the purpose of reliability. In the following, we will hands-on the troubleshooting and performance optimization techniques that we can use directly in our backend project.

Diagnosing and Fixing Stale Data

Usually, stale data is exposed when users report seeing out-of-date content, or when automated tests reveal mismatches between the cache and the database. If we want to catch stale data, we can add extra logging every time the cache is accessed and every time a write occurs.

So, if the cache uses a map or Redis for blog posts, that would be great. Each time a post is updated in the database, log the update and then the cache refresh. When we are doing read operations, make sure we also log the timestamp or version of the cached value. If we compare the logs of writes and reads, we can quickly see if the cache is being properly invalidated or updated.

```
void UpdateBlogPost(const std::string& post_id, const
std::string& new_content) {
    UpdatePostInDatabase(post_id, new_content);
    std::cout << "[DB] Updated post: " << post_id <<
std::endl;
    {
        std::lock_guard<std::mutex> lock(cache_mutex);
        cache[post_id] = new_content;
        std::cout << "[Cache] Updated entry: " << post_id <<
std::endl;
    }
}
std::string GetBlogPost(const std::string& post_id) {
    std::lock_guard<std::mutex> lock(cache_mutex);
    if (cache.find(post_id) != cache.end()) {
        std::cout << "[Cache] Hit for post: " << post_id <<
std::endl;
        return cache[post_id];
    }
    std::cout << "[Cache] Miss for post: " << post_id <<
std::endl;
    std::string post = LoadPostFromDatabase(post_id);
    cache[post_id] = post;
    return post;
}
```

If we keep an eye on these logs, we can spot inconsistencies early on. If the data is still wrong after we have updated or deleted something, check the cache invalidation logic. Also, try adding automated tests that update the data and check for the new value in the cache.

Handling and Observing Cache Stampede

Sometimes, when a hot key expires or is invalidated, a rush of requests may overwhelm the backend database. To detect this, simulate a scenario by setting a short TTL on a popular blog post and then sending a burst of read requests. So, keep an eye on the logs and database metrics for any sudden spikes in load.

To stop this, we need to use a single-flight or locking mechanism, as we talked about before. When we are troubleshooting, it's a good idea to add a flag or mutex that records when a fetch is in progress. Other threads should wait until the first fetch is complete. If we see lots of requests that are getting past the cache for the same key, that's called a stampede. You need to adjust the locking logic and then test again until only one backend fetches from the database during a cache miss.

Measuring Cache Performance

If we need in-depth cache performance, then we need to embed metrics which can gather right inside the service handlers. It can count the cache hits, misses, average lookup time, and time spent fetching from the database. For Redis, we can simply monitor it with the **INFO** command, and the various graph statistics such as hit rate, memory usage, and eviction count can be gathered using Prometheus or Grafana.

Following is a sample program that is using counters:

```
size_t cache_hits = 0, cache_misses = 0;
std::string GetBlogPost(const std::string& post_id) {
    std::lock_guard<std::mutex> lock(cache_mutex);
    if (cache.find(post_id) != cache.end()) {
        ++cache_hits;
        return cache[post_id];
    }
    ++cache_misses;
    std::string post = LoadPostFromDatabase(post_id);
    cache[post_id] = post;
    return post;
}
```

At runtime, we then print the hit rate:

```
double hit_rate = (double)cache_hits / (cache_hits +
cache_misses);
std::cout << "Cache Hit Rate: " << hit_rate * 100 << "%" <<
std::endl;
```

If we want advanced monitoring, we can expose these metrics via an HTTP endpoint or a Prometheus exporter, and after then we can easily visualize in a dashboard.

Summary

All through this chapter, we took a look at how important caching is for improving performance and scalability in Backend systems. We looked at how caching worked as a middleman, letting apps respond to frequent and expensive data requests almost instantly. There were some practical demonstrations on in-memory and database caching, including cache-aside and write-through strategies for keeping cache and data source consistent. We tried out a bunch of different eviction strategies, like LRU, LFU and RR to see how they could be done in C++ to deal with different access patterns. We also had to deal with the challenge of keeping cache consistency, learning how to use techniques like time-to-live, explicit invalidation, and versioning to keep data fresh and accurate.

The chapter finished with some hands-on troubleshooting, where we figured out and fixed problems like stale data, cache stampedes, and node inconsistency. We also learned how to measure and tune cache performance using specific metrics and logging. All these things together gave them a good grounding in how to design, set up and look after high-performance caching layers in modern Backend projects.

Chapter 8: Managing Web Servers with Nginx

We're going to get hands-on with integrating web servers, using Nginx as our main tool in this chapter. To get started, we'll first cover the key role of web servers and the client-server lifecycle. Then, we'll dive into a hands-on, step-by-step setup of Nginx as a reverse proxy, and it'll show us the pros and cons of using it for backend projects. We'll learn how to handle HTTPS traffic like pros, mastering certificate management and secure traffic routing to keep data and client interactions private and trustworthy. Then we'll move on to load balancing for making applications work seamlessly, with clear examples of how to distribute requests and maintain reliability.

As we move forward, we'll be working on making minor adjustments to the SSL/TLS settings to make sure everything is as secure as possible, while also making deployment easier. Finally, we'll look at how to manage both static and dynamic assets efficiently, using Nginx's features for caching, compression, and flexible delivery paths. By the time we reach the end of this chapter, we'll have all the skills we need to design, set up and run a Backend infrastructure that's secure, scalable and ready for production.

Web Servers Overview

For any backend, the web servers stand as the gatekeepers that connect the outside world to the inner workings of our applications. Whether requests originate from browsers, mobile clients, IoT devices, or automated systems, each must first pass through a web server before reaching the backend application. In our project, the web server is often the only component directly exposed to the public internet, entrusted with managing the initial client handshake, enforcing security policies, and orchestrating the distribution of requests.

Request-Response Lifecycle

A web server operates by continuously listening for incoming requests, typically over HTTP or HTTPS. Once a connection is received, the server parses the request to extract critical information such as the target URL, request method (GET, POST, etc.), headers, and payload. Based on this data, the web server determines the best course of action. If the request matches a static resource, such as an image, stylesheet, or prebuilt HTML file, the server retrieves it directly from disk and returns it to the client. For dynamic requests, such as API endpoints or application pages that require logic or database access, the server passes the request to the backend application.

In our project, suppose a client requests the latest blog post. The web server inspects the request and, through its configuration, identifies that this path should be handled by the C++ application. The server might use FastCGI, HTTP proxying, or even a custom gRPC interface to forward the request to the Backend process. The backend receives the request, performs any necessary computation, such as reading from a database or running business logic, and constructs an appropriate response, often in JSON or HTML format. This response is sent back to the web server, which then transmits it to the original client, adding headers for caching, cookies, or security as needed.

Workflow of Web Servers

The web servers follow a structured workflow that begins with network-level connection handling and ends with returning a formatted response to the client. This process can be broken down into several key steps, as outlined below:

1. The web server binds to one or more ports and waits for inbound client connections.
2. Upon receiving data, it interprets the HTTP request, extracts the method, path, and headers, and checks for protocol compliance.
3. Based on its configuration (which can include URL patterns, HTTP methods, or hostnames), the server decides whether to serve a static file, redirect the request, or forward it to a backend handler.
4. For dynamic content, the server forwards the request to the appropriate backend application, in our case, a C++ service, using the configured interface or protocol.
5. The backend generates the response, and the web server receives this output, formats it according to protocol standards, attaches headers, and sends the completed response to the client.

Throughout the process, the web server can log each transaction, collect metrics, and enforce policies such as rate limiting or IP blacklisting.

Advantage of Scalability and Security

One of the big pluses of putting a web server in front of the backend is that it makes for a better architecture. The web server can handle SSL/TLS encryption, so the backend doesn't have to deal with certificate management and secure handshakes directly. It can also handle static content delivery, compress files, and use caching policies to make things faster. When there are lots of backend services running, like microservices or separate API and application servers, the web server is like the central router, load balancer and security enforcer.

In our project, we've configured the web server as the public entry point, which means the backend logic can stay safely behind firewalls and only the web server can access it. This helps to reduce attack surface, makes scaling easier (by balancing traffic across multiple backend instances) and enables the use of advanced features such as reverse proxying, custom routing, and static asset management. All of these help to create a robust, maintainable and high-performing backend environment.

It's all the foundation we need to make sure the Backend project is set up safely, can handle a lot of users, and won't let us down.

Up and Runinng with Nginx

The Nginx has earned its reputation as one of the fastest and most reliable web servers and reverse proxies available for backend deployment. It is designed with performance, scalability, and low resource usage in mind, and well-suited for modern C++ applications that require efficient request routing, load balancing, SSL termination, and seamless serving of both static and dynamic content.

Also, the Nginx is event-driven and asynchronous, which means it can handle thousands of concurrent client connections without becoming a bottleneck. For Backend projects, this capability is invaluable when aiming for minimal latency and maximum throughput, especially under peak load. The Nginx handles direct HTTP(S) traffic, and also excels at proxying requests to backend services through FastCGI, HTTP, or even custom TCP/UDP protocols.

In our project, the Nginx can be easily used to:

- Receive and terminate HTTPS connections, offloading encryption and certificate management from the application code.
- Serve static assets (images, CSS, JavaScript) directly from disk for lightning-fast delivery.
- Proxy API requests to backend C++ processes, enabling application isolation and fine-grained routing.
- Perform load balancing across multiple backend instances for greater reliability and scaling.

Installing Nginx

First, we check if the package lists are up to date, then we install Nginx:

```
sudo apt update
sudo apt install nginx
```

After installation, the Nginx usually starts automatically, and the default configuration listens on port 80. The web server status can be checked with:

```
sudo systemctl status nginx
```

The default Nginx welcome page should appear, confirming a successful installation.

Nginx Configuration

Now, the next step is to tailor Nginx's configuration to fit into our projects requirement. The main configuration file is typically located at **`/etc/nginx/nginx.conf`**, and site-specific configuration files reside in **`/etc/nginx/sites-available/`**.

Now, our backend listens on port 8080 and serves a REST API. So here, we want the Nginx to accept requests on the standard HTTP (or HTTPS) port, then proxy those requests to the backend.

I have outlined the following configuration:

```
server {
    listen 80;
    server_name your-domain.com;
    location / {
        proxy_pass http://localhost:8080;
        proxy_set_header Host $host;
        proxy_set_header X-Real-IP $remote_addr;
        proxy_set_header X-Forwarded-For
$proxy_add_x_forwarded_for;
        proxy_set_header X-Forwarded-Proto $scheme;
    }
    location /static/ {
        alias /var/www/yourproject/static/;
        expires 30d;
        add_header Cache-Control "public, max-age=2592000";
    }
}
```

In the above,

- The **`proxy_pass`** directive tells Nginx to forward all incoming requests to the Backend service running locally.
- The extra headers preserve information about the original request for logging and backend use.
- The **`/static/`** block allows Nginx to serve static files directly from disk, bypassing the backend for optimal speed.

After editing the configuration, we then need to check for syntax errors:

```
sudo nginx -t
```

If all is well, we then reload Nginx to apply changes:

```
sudo systemctl reload nginx
```

After all this, the static resources are served instantly, while all API or dynamic requests are proxied to the C++ application, which could be running as a standalone service, within a container, or behind another layer. This architecture improves security and scalability, and also simplifies certificate management, logging, and performance optimization.

Configuring Reverse Proxy

A reverse proxy server is a key architectural element in modern backend systems, acting as an intermediary between clients and backend applications. In contrast to a traditional forward proxy, which stands between clients and the internet to mediate outbound requests, a reverse proxy sits in front of backend servers, receiving inbound client requests and deciding how to route them to the correct backend process or service.

The most fundamental advantage is that a reverse proxy decouples the public interface of the service from the internal application logic. This separation enables flexible routing, easier scaling, centralized security enforcement, and seamless upgrades or rollbacks of backend components. By handling SSL/TLS encryption, the reverse proxy offloads computationally expensive security operations from the application code. It supports the backend to focus purely on business logic and data processing. A reverse proxy also provides a single, unified endpoint for all client traffic, allowing backend services to reside on private networks and remain inaccessible to external users.

Our backend server runs locally on port 8080. So here, we will ask Nginx to forward all incoming HTTP traffic to this backend. This setup is achieved by editing the server block in Nginx's configuration.

To do this, we first access the configuration file and set up the following:

```
server {
    listen 80;
    server_name myapp.example.com;
    location / {
        proxy_pass http://localhost:8080;
        proxy_set_header Host $host;
        proxy_set_header X-Real-IP $remote_addr;
        proxy_set_header X-Forwarded-For
$proxy_add_x_forwarded_for;
```

```
        proxy_set_header X-Forwarded-Proto $scheme;
    }
}
```

This configuration block tells Nginx to listen for all HTTP requests on port 80 for the specified domain. For every request, the Nginx acts as a reverse proxy by passing it along to the backend service on **localhost:8080**. The extra headers ensure the backend application receives accurate information about the original client's address, protocol, and request origin, which is essential for logging, analytics, or implementing client-specific logic.

After saving the configuration, check it for correctness:

```
sudo nginx -t
```

If the test passes, reload the server to apply changes:

```
sudo systemctl reload nginx
```

To see the reverse proxy in action, we restart the backend application on port 8080. When a user accesses **http://myapp.example.com** in a browser, Nginx intercepts the request, applies any configured rules, and then forwards it to the backend application. The backend responds, Nginx relays the response to the client, and the entire process remains seamless and transparent to the end user.

With this setup, the backend service can be stopped, restarted, or even replaced by another version, all without exposing direct internal details to clients.

Handle HTTPS Traffic

Whenever clients connect over HTTPS, the connection is encrypted, which means that any data sent between the client and server is kept private and can't be intercepted or tampered with by anyone who might want to do us harm. These days, serving traffic over HTTPS is pretty much standard for C++ backend applications, whether we are dealing with browser-based requests, APIs, or even mobile and IoT device interactions. So here, we can centralise the management of SSL/TLS encryption and offload the computational cost from the backend application by terminating HTTPS at the web server or reverse proxy layer. This means that all inbound and outbound traffic is secured, and the backend can focus on core functionality, knowing that all external data has already been protected.

Enabling HTTPS

To enable HTTPS, we first need an SSL/TLS certificate. This certificate can be obtained from a trusted Certificate Authority (CA) or generated as a self-signed certificate for testing or internal purposes.

Once available, the certificate (usually **.crt** or **.pem** file) and its corresponding private key (**.key** file) are placed on the server, typically in a secure directory such as **/etc/ssl/certs/** and **/etc/ssl/private/**.

Listening HTTPS Traffic

The Nginx configuration is then updated to listen for HTTPS traffic on port 443 and to use the certificate files.

Following is a simple example:

```
server {
    listen 443 ssl;
    server_name myapp.example.com;
    ssl_certificate     /etc/ssl/certs/myapp.crt;
    ssl_certificate_key /etc/ssl/private/myapp.key;
    ssl_protocols       TLSv1.2 TLSv1.3;
    ssl_ciphers         HIGH:!aNULL:!MD5;
    location / {
        proxy_pass http://localhost:8080;
        proxy_set_header Host $host;
        proxy_set_header X-Real-IP $remote_addr;
        proxy_set_header X-Forwarded-For
$proxy_add_x_forwarded_for;
        proxy_set_header X-Forwarded-Proto $scheme;
    }
}
```

From the above program,

- The **listen 443 ssl;** directive instructs Nginx to accept HTTPS connections.
- The **ssl_certificate** and **ssl_certificate_key** specify the paths to the certificate and private key.

- The **ssl_protocols** and **ssl_ciphers** lines define strong encryption settings for improved security.
- The proxy settings ensure requests are forwarded securely to the Backend service as with HTTP.

Redirecting HTTP to HTTPS

Just so we know, to keep things secure, it's a good idea to automatically redirect all HTTP traffic to HTTPS. That way, we can be sure that the clients are always connected securely, even if they initially try to access the site over plain HTTP. Add a separate server block for port 80 with a redirect rule:

```
server {
    listen 80;
    server_name myapp.example.com;
    return 301 https://$host$request_uri;
}
```

This above configuration will catch any HTTP request and send a permanent redirect to the equivalent HTTPS URL.

SO overall, when a client visits **https://myapp.example.com**, the Nginx will handle the SSL handshake, decrypt the request, and forward it to the Backend over a secure channel. All the HTTP requests are seamlessly redirected such that, every client session is protected by encryption.

Load Balancing

A load balancer sits between the clients and the backend servers, receiving all incoming requests and intelligently routing them to the backend instances based on a configured strategy. This intermediary layer enables smooth horizontal scaling, where additional backend servers can be added or removed as traffic demands change, without requiring any changes to the client or application logic. It also provides a central point for monitoring health, logging, and applying traffic control policies.

Load Balancing Algorithms and Strategies

There are several algorithms that can be configured for routing traffic to backend servers, each with its own advantages:

Round Robin

In this, the requests are distributed sequentially across all backend servers. This is simple and effective when backend nodes have similar capabilities and resource profiles.

Least Connections

In this algorithm, the new requests are sent to the server handling the fewest active connections, which helps balance the load in scenarios where some requests take longer to process.

IP Hash

The client's IP address determines which backend server handles the request, as it assures that the requests from the same client are consistently routed to the same backend for the benefit of session persistence.

The Nginx supports all the above algorithms, with support to fine-tune the control over traffic distribution.

Configuring Load Balancer

To set up Nginx as a load balancer, we need to define a group of backend servers (also known as an upstream) and specify the load balancing algorithm. For example, we will assume that we've got our C++ app set up on three servers running on ports 8081, 8082 and 8083.

The following Nginx configuration implements a round robin load balancer:

```
upstream backend_pool {
    server 127.0.0.1:8081;
    server 127.0.0.1:8082;
    server 127.0.0.1:8083;
}
server {
    listen 80;
    server_name myapp.example.com;
    location / {
        proxy_pass http://backend_pool;
        proxy_set_header Host $host;
        proxy_set_header X-Real-IP $remote_addr;
        proxy_set_header X-Forwarded-For
$proxy_add_x_forwarded_for;
```

```
        proxy_set_header X-Forwarded-Proto $scheme;
    }
}
```

To use the least connections method, simply add **`least_conn;`** in the upstream block:

```
upstream backend_pool {
    least_conn;
    server 127.0.0.1:8081;
    server 127.0.0.1:8082;
    server 127.0.0.1:8083;
}
```

For session persistence using IP hash:

```
upstream backend_pool {
    ip_hash;
    server 127.0.0.1:8081;
    server 127.0.0.1:8082;
    server 127.0.0.1:8083;
}
```

Once we've got load balancing sorted, it's a piece of cake to scale the backend. We just add new servers to the pool in the configuration and traffic gets distributed automatically. We can perform rolling upgrades and blue-green deployments by draining traffic from one backend at a time, updating or restarting the server, and then returning it to service, all without disrupting our clients.

SSL Configuration

The SSL/TLS configuration stands at the heart of securing client-server communications in any modern backend deployment. A well-configured SSL/TLS layer not only encrypts data in transit, protecting it from eavesdropping and tampering, but also forms the basis for user trust and compliance with contemporary security standards. In our project, the handling of SSL/TLS can easily centralize the management, minimize the attack surface, and also can streamline the delivery of secure APIs.

Acquiring SSL/TLS Certificates

The certificates are typically issued by trusted Certificate Authorities (CAs), such as Let's Encrypt (free and automated) or commercial providers. For internal use or testing, we can generate the self-signed certificates, though browsers will mark these as untrusted.

The certificates consist of a public certificate file (often **.crt** or **.pem**) and a private key file (**.key**). Both files should be stored securely on the server, with strict permissions to prevent unauthorized access to the private key. We can simply place them in directories like **/etc/ssl/certs/** and **/etc/ssl/private/** for consistency and safety.

Now, to activate SSL/TLS in Nginx, we configure the server block to listen on port 443 and specify the certificate files.

Following is a practical configuration, integrating strong protocols and cipher suites for enhanced security:

```
server {
    listen 443 ssl http2;
    server_name myapp.example.com;
    ssl_certificate     /etc/ssl/certs/myapp.crt;
    ssl_certificate_key /etc/ssl/private/myapp.key;
    ssl_protocols       TLSv1.2 TLSv1.3;
    ssl_ciphers         'ECDHE-ECDSA-AES256-GCM-SHA384:ECDHE-
RSA-AES256-GCM-SHA384:ECDHE-ECDSA-CHACHA20-POLY1305:ECDHE-RSA-
CHACHA20-POLY1305:ECDHE-ECDSA-AES128-GCM-SHA256:ECDHE-RSA-
AES128-GCM-SHA256';
    ssl_prefer_server_ciphers on;
    ssl_session_cache   shared:SSL:10m;
    ssl_session_timeout 10m;
    ssl_session_tickets off;
    add_header Strict-Transport-Security "max-age=31536000;
includeSubDomains" always;
    location / {
        proxy_pass http://localhost:8080;
        proxy_set_header Host $host;
        proxy_set_header X-Real-IP $remote_addr;
```

```
        proxy_set_header X-Forwarded-For
$proxy_add_x_forwarded_for;
        proxy_set_header X-Forwarded-Proto $scheme;
    }
}
```

This configuration enables HTTP/2, it limits allowed protocols to secure versions (TLS 1.2 and 1.3), sets robust cipher preferences, and also configures the HTTP Strict Transport Security (HSTS) to enforce encrypted connections for all future requests.

If we are thinking to make use of Let's Encrypt, then there are tools like **`certbot`** which can automate both the issuance and renewal of such certificates. We can also have a common cron job to notify us, such that the certificates never expire.

Testing SSL/TLS Configuration

After the successful configuration, we must test, if there are any syntax errors:

```
sudo nginx -t
```

After this, reload the Nginx to apply changes:

```
sudo systemctl reload nginx
```

And then verify the SSL/TLS operation by visiting **`https://myapp.example.com`** in a browser and inspect the security certificate. We can make use of various tool that are available, like SSL Labs' SSL Server Test. We can use it to grade the server's security, flag outdated protocols, or suggest improvements.

Managing Static and Dynamic Assets

Every backend application, especially those serving web clients or APIs, must efficiently deliver both static and dynamic assets to users. **Static assets** are files that do not change frequently, such as images, CSS, JavaScript, fonts, and downloadable documents. **Dynamic assets** are resources generated in real time by the backend application, often tailored to each request; these may include personalized HTML pages, rendered templates, API responses, or files assembled from live data.

For Backend projects, effectively managing both static and dynamic assets is crucial for maximizing performance, reliability, and user experience. The configuration of the web server, typically Nginx, determines how these assets are served, cached, and protected from misuse or excessive load.

Serving Static Assets

The thing that Nginx does best is serving static content really quickly and using hardly any CPU or memory. If we set up Nginx to handle static files straight from the filesystem, the backend apps won't have to deal with these resources, so they can focus on dynamic logic.

A common configuration for static files looks like this:

```
server {
    listen 80;
    server_name myapp.example.com;
    location /static/ {
        alias /var/www/myapp/static/;
        expires 30d;
        add_header Cache-Control "public, max-age=2592000";
    }
    location / {
        proxy_pass http://localhost:8080;
        proxy_set_header Host $host;
        proxy_set_header X-Real-IP $remote_addr;
        proxy_set_header X-Forwarded-For
$proxy_add_x_forwarded_for;
        proxy_set_header X-Forwarded-Proto $scheme;
    }
}
```

With this configuration, any request to a path beginning with **`/static/`** will be served directly from the **`/var/www/myapp/static/`** directory, bypassing the Backend entirely. The **`expires`** and **`Cache-Control`** headers instruct browsers to cache these assets for a month, dramatically reducing repeated requests and speeding up user interactions.

Delivering Dynamic Assets

The dynamic assets, such as rendered web pages or API data, require processing by the backend application for each request. Nginx, acting as a reverse proxy, forwards these requests to the Backend for processing.

For example, when a client requests a user dashboard or a freshly generated report, the Nginx server matches the URL to the root location (/), forwards it to the backend, and then relays the backend's response to the client. This keeps dynamic and static asset delivery paths clear and optimized, such that the dynamic requests receive computation and security needed, while static files are always delivered at peak speed.

Optimizing Asset Delivery

For optimization, we can enable the compression with:

```
gzip on;
gzip_types text/css application/javascript application/json;
gzip_min_length 1024;
```

By delegating static asset delivery to Nginx, the backend projects not only gain a significant performance boost but also simplify application logic. The backend remains focused on generating dynamic content and business logic, while Nginx ensures fast, reliable, and scalable delivery of all assets.

In summary, managing static and dynamic assets efficiently with Nginx creates a seamless user experience, reduces server load, and supports the robust scaling of Backend services. This approach forms a cornerstone of modern web application deployment, uniting speed, security, and maintainability in every release.

Summary

During this chapter, we took a look at how web servers are key to backend architecture, and how they act as the gateway between clients and application logic. We took a look at how web servers handle requests, manage connections, and provide a basic layer for delivering both static and dynamic content in our project. We learned the benefits of implementing a reverse proxy, such as centralised security, SSL offloading and flexible routing, and then set up Nginx to manage HTTPS traffic, secure certificates and ensure every client session remained encrypted.

The chapter also covered using Nginx as a load balancer for distributing requests across multiple backend instances. There was a lot of focus on SSL/TLS best practices, which really highlighted how crucial strong encryption and automated certificate management are. At last, we looked at how to serve static and dynamic assets efficiently, and we optimised Nginx settings for caching, compression and access control.

Chapter 9: Testing C++ Backend

The aim of this chapter is to establish a solid base for quality and reliability in C++ backend development by focusing on systematic testing practices. We'll kick things off by looking at the importance of testing and how it helps keep backend systems stable and resilient. We'll take a look at the top C++ testing frameworks out there, compare their features, and see why Google Test is going to be our go-to choice for both small and large projects. Then, it'll walk us through the nitty-gritty of setting up and configuring Google Test, making sure our test environment is seamlessly hooked up to our build workflow. We'll develop unit tests that proactively prevent data loss and catch subtle bugs before they reach production.

We'll be expanding the scope, so we'll be writing integration tests for core backend components like MongoDB and gRPC. We'll be simulating real-world interactions and making sure data flows accurately between services. Then the last part will be about continuous testing and test automation, which will give us the know-how to set up pipelines where every code change is validated straight away, speeding up development cycles and making them safer.

C++ Testing Frameworks: Doctest and Google Test

The concept of testing matters deeply in backend projects because the consequences of errors are often severe and wide-ranging. A minor bug in a data handling routine can lead to silent data loss, security vulnerabilities, or system downtime that affects thousands of users. In distributed systems, where components interact across networks and services, even simple miscommunications between APIs or database layers can snowball into complex, hard-to-diagnose failures. So here, a disciplined testing culture can help teams to prevent these issues from lurking undetected, instead surfacing them early during development or continuous integration.

Exploring Doctest and Google Test

In the world of Backend development, adopting a solid testing framework is critical for creating maintainable, reliable software. Among the available tools, **Doctest** and **Google Test** have both emerged as popular and effective choices, each offering unique advantages for backend engineers.

Doctest

The **Doctest** is celebrated for its simplicity and minimalism. This tool is inspired by Python's doctest module, which allows developers to write concise tests that can live in the same source files as the code they validate. Its lightweight design means almost no build or runtime overhead, making it ideal for quick checks, single-header integration, and test-driven development in smaller or embedded C++ projects. The Doctest emphasizes readability, instant compilation, and straightforward usage, lowering the barrier for introducing tests into any codebase.

Google Test

The **Google Test** (or GTest), by contrast, is a comprehensive and feature-rich framework tailored for large-scale, complex C++ projects. As an open-source offering from Google, it brings robust support for a wide range of assertions, parameterized and typed tests, advanced test fixtures, and seamless integration with continuous integration pipelines. The Google Test encourages the separation of test and implementation code, supports rich reporting, and works comfortably alongside modern build systems like CMake. Its maturity and strong community backing have made it the default choice for many production-grade backend systems, open-source libraries, and enterprise codebases.

Choosing Google Test

While both frameworks serve the C++ ecosystem well, the **Google Test** stands out as the most favourable tool, especially for our backend project. And, the reasons are both practical and strategic as below:

- The Google Test scales smoothly as the project grows, supporting everything from basic unit checks to complex integration suites.
- Its expressive assertion macros and powerful fixtures accommodate the sophisticated data flows and interactions that are common in backend applications.
- It's built-in support for parameterized testing, test discovery, and result reporting simplifies the maintenance of large test suites and supports automation via CI/CD.
- And finally, this tool is well documented, actively maintained, and widely used in industry. It guarantees the long-term support and a wealth of resources for troubleshooting or advanced use cases.

If we go for Google Test, our backend project will get a good, industry-standard testing tool that ticks all the boxes for robust C++ development. We'll be setting up and using Google Test as the basis for all our automated testing, which'll give the team the confidence to build, refactor and scale safely and efficiently.

Install Google Test

So, to get automated testing going in our backend project, we're going to start by adding Google Test to our repository. If we're working on a Git-based project, we open our terminal in the project's root folder and set up Google Test as a submodule. So, when we run the submodule command, we get the full source in a special directory in our codebase.

```
git submodule add https://github.com/google/googletest.git
third_party/googletest

git submodule update --init --recursive
```

This ensures our backend and the test framework always travel together, no matter where the repository is cloned or built. If our workflow does not involve submodules, downloading and extracting the release archive into a local directory achieves the same effect.

Once the Google Test lives within our project directory, we can adapt our build system to recognize and build the framework. Since CMake is the build system of choice for most C++ backends, we open our **`CMakeLists.txt`** and instruct CMake to include the Google Test source tree.

In the following snippet, we link the framework to our test binary:

```
add_subdirectory(third_party/googletest)
add_executable(backend_tests tests/test_main.cpp)
target_link_libraries(backend_tests gtest gtest_main)
enable_testing()
add_test(NAME BackendTests COMMAND backend_tests)
```

If our test cases grow, we add more source files to the **`tests`** directory and simply list them as additional sources for the test binary.

Now, in our project root, we then set up a build folder to keep everything tidy, generate our build files, and compile both application and tests:

```
mkdir build
cd build
cmake ..
make
```

Now, when compilation completes, the test runner is ready for action. To run all tests, we simply execute:

```
ctest
```

The CMake discovers every test case, and Google Test reports on the outcomes. The failures are quite easy to identify, and the results also show us immediately, if any further work is needed. The Google Test becomes a living safety net, running locally, in our code reviews, and on every automated build.

Perform Unit Testing for Data Loss

It's really important to keep data accurate, so if we make a mistake when saving, updating or retrieving information, we might lose records, break relationships or miss out fields, which can mess up users and make people distrust the app. So, unit tests are our first and best protection against data loss. These tests don't just catch the obvious bugs; they actively confirm that each individual function or component preserves every piece of information, even in edge cases. We build focused tests for all data operations, which creates a living shield around our project's most valuable asset.

Designing Safe Storage Component

We first consider a core component of our backend, a simple storage system for blog posts, just to be sure that whenever we save a post, the title, content, and unique ID are all preserved without loss, truncation, or unintentional overwriting.

So here, we will design our data structure and storage class as follows:

```
struct BlogPost {
    std::string id;
    std::string title;
    std::string content;
};
class BlogStorage {
public:
    void StoreBlogPost(const BlogPost& post) {
        posts_[post.id] = post;
    }
    BlogPost GetBlogPost(const std::string& id) const {
        auto it = posts_.find(id);
        if (it != posts_.end()) {
            return it->second;
        }
        return BlogPost{};
    }
private:
    std::unordered_map<std::string, BlogPost> posts_;
```

```
};
```

From this, each blog post is uniquely identified by an ID, and all posts are stored in an internal map. The retrieval method ensures that when an ID is provided, the entire blog post, with all fields, can be recovered as it was stored.

Writing Unit Tests

Now that we've got our storage logic sorted, we'll move on to writing Google Test unit tests to make sure the data is intact. Basically, we start by building a test that saves a sample post, retrieves it, and makes sure that none of the characters have been lost or changed.

```
#include <gtest/gtest.h>
TEST(BlogStorageTest, StoresAndRetrievesAllFieldsCorrectly) {
    BlogStorage storage;
    BlogPost original_post = {"101", "Unit Testing for Data
Loss", "Each character matters here."};
    storage.StoreBlogPost(original_post);
    BlogPost loaded_post = storage.GetBlogPost("101");
    EXPECT_EQ(loaded_post.id, "101");
    EXPECT_EQ(loaded_post.title, "Unit Testing for Data
Loss");
    EXPECT_EQ(loaded_post.content, "Each character matters
here.");
}
```

From the above, the test directly verifies that every attribute, ID, title, and content, is faithfully preserved during storage and retrieval. This gives immediate feedback if any part of our logic introduces data loss, such as empty fields, misaligned assignment, or accidental truncation.

Handling Empty Fields and Large Content

Also, data loss can happen in less obvious situations. If a post has an empty title or very large content, what happens? To do this, we add more unit tests to explore these scenarios:

```
TEST(BlogStorageTest, HandlesEmptyFieldsWithoutDataLoss) {
    BlogStorage storage;
    BlogPost empty_post = {"102", "", ""};
```

```
    storage.StoreBlogPost(empty_post);
    BlogPost loaded_post = storage.GetBlogPost("102");
    EXPECT_EQ(loaded_post.title, "");
    EXPECT_EQ(loaded_post.content, "");
}
TEST(BlogStorageTest, StoresAndRetrievesLargeContent) {
    BlogStorage storage;
    std::string large_content(10000, 'A');
    BlogPost big_post = {"103", "Big", large_content};
    storage.StoreBlogPost(big_post);
    BlogPost loaded_post = storage.GetBlogPost("103");
    EXPECT_EQ(loaded_post.content.size(), 10000);
    EXPECT_EQ(loaded_post.content[0], 'A');
}
```

These tests confirm that our backend logic gracefully accepts empty fields and is robust enough to handle large data blocks, never dropping or corrupting the information.

After running these tests with our regular test command, if any test fails, the output clearly points to which field or logic step allowed data to slip through. This feedback allows us to correct problems early, before they have any chance to affect real users or production databases.

Integration Testing for MongoDB and gRPC

We know how unit tests protect individual functions and classes? But integration testing makes sure that the different parts of our backend actually work together as expected. The reality is that in a modern C++ backend, real-world functionality is rarely found on its own. Instead, backend components talk to external systems, like databases and APIs, and use protocols like gRPC to handle complex data flows. We can't do without integration tests when our project involves interactions with services like MongoDB for storing data and gRPC for communicating between services. When we simulate realistic workflows, we make sure that not only does the internal logic work properly, but we also check that the connections are correct, that the data is arranged in the right order, and that information is moving from one place to another across different boundaries in the right way.

Setting up Testable Environment

To begin integration testing, we establish an environment where a test instance of MongoDB is running, either locally or within a container. Our backend is configured to connect to this instance, using a dedicated test database to prevent interference with production data. Simultaneously, the backend service exposes gRPC endpoints, implemented with libraries such as **grpc-cpp**, and is launched so test clients can interact with it programmatically. The Google Test framework, already part of our project, allows us to write and execute integration tests that communicate directly with both MongoDB and gRPC endpoints.

Testing End-to-End Persistence with MongoDB

Now here, suppose our backend stores blog posts in MongoDB through a method like **SavePostToMongoDB**. The integration test will insert a document via the C++ logic, retrieve it back, and confirm that the fields are preserved throughout the process.

We can then set up a special MongoDB URI that targets a non-production database, such as **mongodb://localhost:27017/testdb**. The test will create a post, save it, and then fetch it directly from the database to check that nothing is lost or altered in translation.

```
TEST(MongoDBIntegrationTest, SavesAndRetrievesPostCorrectly) {
    BlogPost post = {"201", "Integration Testing", "Checking
MongoDB persistence."};
    BlogStorage storage("mongodb://localhost:27017/testdb");
    storage.SavePostToMongoDB(post);
    BlogPost retrieved = storage.GetPostFromMongoDB("201");
    EXPECT_EQ(retrieved.id, "201");
    EXPECT_EQ(retrieved.title, "Integration Testing");
    EXPECT_EQ(retrieved.content, "Checking MongoDB
persistence.");
}
```

This test confirms that data flows smoothly from the Backend into MongoDB and returns uncorrupted. It is proving that both serialization and deserialization, as well as database configuration, are functioning correctly.

Verifying gRPC Service Interactions

The integration testing with gRPC involves launching the backend service and then creating a gRPC client in our test suite that sends real requests over the network interface. For instance, if our backend exposes a CreatePost RPC endpoint, we craft a test that builds a gRPC client, sends a request, and checks the response for correctness.

```
TEST(GRPCIntegrationTest, CreatePostViaGRPC) {
    auto channel = grpc::CreateChannel("localhost:50051",
grpc::InsecureChannelCredentials());
    std::unique_ptr<BlogService::Stub> stub =
BlogService::NewStub(channel);
    BlogPostRequest request;
    request.set_id("301");
    request.set_title("gRPC Integration");
    request.set_content("Testing gRPC workflow.");
    BlogPostReply reply;
    grpc::ClientContext context;
    grpc::Status status = stub->CreatePost(&context, request,
&reply);
    EXPECT_TRUE(status.ok());
    EXPECT_EQ(reply.id(), "301");
    EXPECT_EQ(reply.title(), "gRPC Integration");
    EXPECT_EQ(reply.content(), "Testing gRPC workflow.");
}
```

From the above, it ensures that the service endpoint is available, the serialization formats match, and the backend logic correctly processes gRPC requests from real clients. Any change in API contracts, serialization, or network configuration will surface immediately in these integration checks.

All these tests catch subtle bugs that only appear when systems communicate, such as connection issues, schema mismatches, or broken endpoint implementations. With adding new endpoints or integrating new data stores, we can expand the integration tests to keep pace with its functionality and scale.

Integrating Testing with Build Pipelines

As time goes on, we'll be adding new features to our project, which could mean breaking existing logic or introducing small data errors. So, continuous testing is when every code change, no matter how small, triggers a new round of automated tests. This way, any problems can be spotted straight away, not days or weeks down the line. We make sure that the whole backend is regularly and reliably tested through automation, which is the foundation of fast and consistent releases.

So here, we connect our test suite to an automated build pipeline. This pipeline can be managed by platforms such as GitHub Actions, GitLab CI, Jenkins, or any other system supporting CMake-based C++ builds. When a developer pushes code or creates a pull request, the system automatically pulls the latest changes, configures the environment, builds the project, including all test binaries, and then runs the full suite of Google Test cases.

In our GitHub Actions project repository, we place a file to define the workflow such as **.github/workflows/ci.yml**:

```
name: C++ Backend CI
on: [push, pull_request]
jobs:
  build-and-test:
    runs-on: ubuntu-latest
    steps:
    - uses: actions/checkout@v3
    - name: Install dependencies
      run: sudo apt-get update && sudo apt-get install -y
cmake g++ libgtest-dev
    - name: Build
      run: |
        mkdir build
        cd build
        cmake ..
        make
    - name: Run Tests
      run: |
        cd build
        ctest --output-on-failure
```

Now, from this configuration, every time changes are introduced, the workflow fetches the latest code, installs the needed build tools and libraries, then builds the application and its tests. The test runner reports the results, flagging any failures. This feedback appears instantly on every code review, allowing the team to fix errors before code is merged.

As the backend grows, so does the need for new tests. When new features, bug fixes, or dependencies are added, corresponding tests are created or updated. The automation pipeline will always run the full suite. Over time, this living test suite becomes the project's greatest asset, enabling rapid iteration, fearless refactoring, and high-confidence releases in every stage of backend development.

Summary

As we saw in this chapter, it's really important to test Backend systems systematically if we want them to be healthy and grow. We started by getting to grips with why testing is so important for reliable software, especially when we think about the risks of data loss or tiny logic errors having major consequences in production environments. We then set up Google Test in our codebase, configured CMake and project directories to make testing a seamless part of development. We had some practical examples that showed how to write and run unit tests to protect against data loss.

We moved further to integration testing, connecting our C++ code to external systems like MongoDB and gRPC, and validated the whole workflow through realistic test scenarios. The chapter ended with everyone agreeing to carry on with continuous testing and automation, which means the test suite is now part of the build pipelines so that every time there's a code change, it's immediately checked.

Chapter 10: Deploying Application

Now, in this chapter, we're going to take our Backend project from a build artifact to a live, cloud-hosted application that's ready for real users and production workloads. We'll start with a thorough list of things to do before we deploy, making sure we cover all the essential tasks to make sure our application is fully configured, secure, and environment-agnostic. Then we'll move step by step through containerising the backend using a best-practice Dockerfile, showing us how to build and test the container so we can be absolutely confident before deploying.

Basically, this chapter will walk us through setting up the app on AWS Elastic Beanstalk, using both the AWS CLI and Elastic Beanstalk CLI to make the process as smooth as possible, configuring secrets, environment variables, and managing persistent storage. We'll get really good at checking things and keeping an eye on them as we learn to test endpoints, check health dashboards, look at logs, and use AWS CloudWatch to see how our application is doing. At last, we'll look at what to do after deployment, like updating, rolling back and scaling the application. This'll give us a strong set of tools to use.

Deployment Checklist

At professional backend teams, we never leave deployment preparation to guesswork. Every time a new project is released, developers rely on a strict, step-by-step process to make sure the move from development to live systems is smooth, reliable and secure. Usually, deployment is seen as a key part of the development process, not something that happens at the end, so it's good to build readiness checks into daily routines and automation pipelines. Even the most experienced teams never trust unverified code or configurations. They always verify the build, synchronise environments and run a set of pre-deployment validations to catch hidden issues early.

The preparation stage starts well before deployment day. Teams are always testing to make sure that every build can be reliably produced from the source, using clean environments that mirror production. All environment variables, secrets, and configuration files are managed separately from the application code, so we can be sure that sensitive values are never hardcoded or accidentally leaked. Any changes to the database, like adding new tables or changing schemas, are treated as versioned migrations. These are always run in staging before going live. Things like images, scripts, or compiled frontends are also gathered and prepared for the right place, so that no missing or out-of-date files mess up the application when it's launched. This careful approach, with its checklists and automation, is what makes the difference between good engineering teams and those that really hit the mark.

Deployment Preparation Stages

Validating Builds

A production deployment begins with confidence in the build, and every binary or container must be reproducible from version-controlled source code. The teams typically use continuous integration pipelines to build the application in a clean environment, running the full test suite as described in previous chapters. The artifacts produced, executables, libraries, or Docker images, are tagged with version numbers or commit hashes, such that every deployment can be traced back to its source.

Now here, before moving forward, we need to run a final build in a fresh environment, such as a CI agent or Docker container, then checking for missing dependencies, and the platform mismatches, or the configuration drift.

Environment Variables and Configuration Management

The applications are rarely deployed with static configuration. Instead, there are settings such as database URIs, API keys, ports, logging levels, and feature flags are externalized as environment variables or mounted configuration files. In our project, we might use environment variable libraries like **`std::getenv`** or **`Boost`**, or load settings from YAML, JSON, or INI files provided at runtime. The environment variables ensure the same build can run in multiple environments, staging, production, or development, without code changes.

After this, we gather all the required variables in a template **`.env`** and review them before deployment. Now here, it is very common to have missing or outdated configuration and could cause of downtime, so hence each variable needs to be checked for completeness and accuracy.

Secret Handling

It's no secret that we should never put stuff like API tokens, database passwords or encryption keys in source control. Instead, secrets are injected into the runtime environment through secure systems like AWS Secrets Manager, Docker secrets, or environment variables set in deployment orchestration tools. But before we deploy it, we make sure that all the secrets are there, valid, and only accessible by the application process. There are automated scripts and tools for infrastructure as code like provision and rotate secrets securely.

Database Migrations

It's a simple process: any schema change to the backend database, like adding a column, updating an index, or altering a constraint, is packaged as a versioned migration script. And for C++ projects using databases like MongoDB, tools like Flyway, Liquibase, or custom migration runners are used to apply changes safely. We test the migration in a staging environment to make sure it'll work and that no data will be lost or corrupted. When we're rolling it out, we run migrations as a step before launching the new application, just to make sure the backend and database are in sync.

Static Assets Preparation

All the static files (images, CSS, JavaScript) are collected, versioned and staged in the deployment package. With a CDN or static file server, assets are uploaded before the backend is updated. The deployment checklist confirms that the asset directories match the expected structure and no required files are missing. As for cloud environments, we can use storage services like Amazon S3 to store and serve static content.

Deployment Readiness Checklist

Before deployment begins, we pause and confirm the following:

- The build passes all automated tests and was created in a clean environment.
- All configuration variables, environment files, and secrets are present, accurate, and securely managed.
- Database migration scripts have been tested in staging and are ready for production.
- Static assets are gathered, versioned, and uploaded where necessary.
- The deployment package is tagged and traceable to a specific commit or release.

All the above steps helps us to position our Backend project for a successful and stress-free deployment.

Containerizing Backend

Creating Production-Ready Dockerfile

Our backend project is following a very clear structure, in which all the source code resides in the **`src/`** directory, a **`CMakeLists.txt`** file sits at the root, and any static assets are found in the **`static/`** folder. So here, we will enable smooth deployment and consistent operation across all environments. And, for this, we will package our application into a Docker container using a multi-stage Dockerfile.

The first stage of our Dockerfile sets up a build environment with all required development tools. It pulls from the official Ubuntu 22.04 image, installs **`build-essential`** and **`cmake`**, and copies our entire project into **`/app`**. The application is built with CMake, producing the final executable **`my_backend_app`** within the **`/app/build/`** directory.

The second stage starts from a fresh Ubuntu image and copies only the compiled binary and the static asset directory. By doing this, we avoid shipping development tools or unnecessary files in production.

Given below is our confident, production-grade Dockerfile for the backend project:

```
# Stage 1: Build the C++ backend application
FROM ubuntu:22.04 AS builder
RUN apt-get update && \
```

```
    apt-get install -y build-essential cmake
WORKDIR /app
COPY . .
RUN cmake -S . -B build
RUN cmake --build build --target my_backend_app
# Stage 2: Assemble the runtime image
FROM ubuntu:22.04
WORKDIR /app
# Copy only the necessary files from the builder stage
COPY --from=builder /app/build/my_backend_app .
COPY --from=builder /app/static ./static
# Set required environment variables for production
ENV ENVIRONMENT=production
# Expose the backend service port
EXPOSE 8080
# Launch the application by default
ENTRYPOINT ["./my_backend_app"]
```

This above shown Dockerfile in place tells us confidently that it has encapsulated the build and runtime requirements, and therefore confirming us the portability and repeatability in every environment.

Building Docker Container Locally

To verify that our backend runs flawlessly in its container, we build the image locally. From the project root directory (where the Dockerfile and **CMakeLists.txt** reside), we run:

```
docker build -t my-backend:latest .
```

The docker processes each instruction, setting up the build environment, compiling the application, and packaging only the essentials into the final image. Once the build completes, the container is ready for local testing, and for this, we start the container and then map the internal service port 8080 to our local system:

```
docker run --rm -p 8080:8080 -e ENVIRONMENT=production my-backend:latest
```

From the above, the container is running and we can interact with our backend as we would in production. This includes sending HTTP requests, accessing static assets, and monitoring logs for correct startup messages and behavior. If the backend relies on external services, such as a database, those can be run in parallel containers or with Docker Compose to mirror the complete runtime environment.

In cases where troubleshooting is needed, we need to launch the container in interactive mode and then accordingly we can inspect the environment directly:

```
docker run -it --entrypoint /bin/bash my-backend:latest
```

This will allow us to confirm paths, configuration, and file presence before ever shipping the image to the cloud or a registry.

From the above entire process, the resulting Docker image is lightweight, secure, and ready for cloud deployment. It gives us the exact representation of the application and assets built from our source. With containerization mastered, every future release can be tested, shipped, and scaled without ambiguity or surprise.

AWS Deployment with Elastic Beanstalk and ECS

AWS Elastic Beanstalk Overview

The Elastic Beanstalk from AWS is a fully managed deployment service that makes it straightforward to launch, manage, and scale modern backend applications. It abstracts away most of the infrastructure details, allowing us to focus on our Backend and its configuration rather than worrying about manual provisioning of virtual machines, networking, or scaling policies. So if we make use of Elastic Beanstalk, then our Dockerized backend can be deployed with just a few commands, and AWS does take care of rolling updates, load balancing, monitoring, and integration with other cloud services, as well.

We also need to remember that the Elastic Beanstalk supports Docker natively. Hence, we may keep in mind that it can be an excellent choice for deploying the containerized C++ backend. With just a simple configuration and leveraging the AWS CLI tools, we can move our tested local image into a robust, production-ready cloud environment. In addition, the Elastic Beanstalk also allows us to pass environment variables, access AWS-managed secrets, and attach persistent storage volumes, all essential features for professional backend operations.

Setting up Elastic Beanstalk (EB)

The AWS CLI is a universal tool for all AWS operations, while the EB CLI is designed specifically for EB workflows.

To install the AWS CLI, we use:

```
pip install awscli --upgrade --user
```

For the EB CLI, the installation can be done as follows:

```
pip install awsebcli --upgrade --user
```

Once both tools are installed, we can configure our AWS credentials to grant permission for deployments:

```
aws configure
```

This above command prompts for AWS Access Key, Secret Key, default region (for example, **`us-east-1`**), and output format. These credentials should be associated with a user who has EB, EC2, ECR, and S3 permissions.

Preparing Dockerized App for Beanstalk

The EB expects the application code and its Dockerfile to be in the root directory of the deployment package. We need to ensure that our backend's **`Dockerfile`**, application binary, and supporting files (**`static/`**, etc.) are present at the root of the project folder. If we use a **`docker-compose.yml`** (for multi-container applications), the Beanstalk can support that as well.

So here, to initialize the EB application, we execute:

```
eb init
```

From this, we then choose the appropriate region and select the Docker platform. If prompted, we set the application name and configure SSH access for troubleshooting and log retrieval.

Deploying Application on AWS EB

After the environment is initialized, we then create and launch the EB environment:

```
eb create my-backend-env
```

The Beanstalk automatically detects the Dockerfile, builds the container, and provisions the infrastructure (EC2 instances, load balancer, security groups, and more). The deployment output provides a public endpoint where our application will be accessible once the environment is healthy.

So, to update the application after changes, we simply run:

```
eb deploy
```

This command packages, uploads, and redeploys the latest version to the environment, applying rolling updates without downtime.

Integrating Environment Variables, Secrets, & Persistent Storage

The EB makes it straightforward to pass environment variables directly into the running containers. So here, we configure these using the CLI or AWS Console:

```
eb setenv ENVIRONMENT=production API_KEY=your_api_key
DB_URI=your_db_uri
```

These variables are available to the application at runtime, supporting configuration without hardcoding sensitive values.

For secrets, the AWS recommends using services like AWS Secrets Manager or SSM Parameter Store. Our application retrieves secrets at startup using the AWS SDK or by referencing environment variables mapped to secrets. If persistent storage is required (for file uploads, logs, or other data that must outlive container restarts), so here, we then attach the Elastic Block Store (EBS) volumes. The Beanstalk environment can also be customized with **`.ebextensions`** YAML files to mount volumes or run initialization commands.

Confirming Deployment

Once the deployment is complete, we can then test the public endpoint provided by Beanstalk. This ensures us that the backend is responding as expected. The AWS CloudWatch provides real-time metrics for health, resource usage, and logs. If such issues arise, then the **`eb logs`** retrieves logs for debugging.

All these above steps takes our Dockerized Backend to a robust, cloud-hosted production deployment, which is complete with environment management, secrets integration, and reliable monitoring.

Monitoring Deployment

Live Deployment Verification

The verification process begins by retrieving the public endpoint that AWS provides for our EB environment. This endpoint is visible in the output of the **`eb create`** command, or it can be found in the AWS Management Console under the EB dashboard for the specific environment.

So here, we start by visiting the public URL in a browser or by issuing a request from the terminal using **`curl`**:

```
curl http://<beanstalk-environment-url>
```

If the backend exposes a health endpoint (such as **`/health`**), we can request that path directly:

```
curl http://<beanstalk-environment-url>/health
```

If the output gives a successful HTTP 200 response, or an application-specific healthy message, then we can say that the application is up and processing requests.

Reviewing AWS EB Health Dashboards

Let's go to the AWS Management Console and access the EB service to get a broader view of deployment health. Just select the environment and we will be shown a dashboard with real-time health status, environment metrics, instance counts and deployment history, without any long manual efforts of dashboard configuration.

If we click on the "Health" tab, we will get immediate feedback on whether instances are healthy, degraded, or experiencing failures. And if the status is anything but "Ok", the dashboard will highlight the reasons, like failed deployments, application crashes or resource exhaustion. Then there's the "Monitoring" tab, which has charts on CPU utilisation, memory and request latency.

To take a closer look, we can use the EB CLI to fetch environment logs straight away:

```
eb logs
```

This command downloads the most recent logs from all instances, including application output, web server logs, and deployment event logs. If we read these logs carefully, we will be able to confirm about the backend started successfully, or it is listening on the correct port, and that there are no configuration errors or runtime crashes.

Inspecting Application and Container Logs

As well as looking at environmental health, it's really important to keep an eye on application-level and container logs. In the Beanstalk dashboard, the "Logs" section gives us access to recent logs. And for Dockerized applications, the Beanstalk collects standard output and error streams, so any **`std::cout`**, **`std::cerr`**, or log file output generated by the backend is captured here.

We can use this to check that environment variables are loaded, startup routines are complete, and there are no runtime warnings or errors. Any odd things that go wrong or if it fails to startup properly, we can see straight away by looking through these log files.

Setting up CloudWatch Monitoring

Just so we know, we can use AWS CloudWatch with EB and it'll give us all the info we need on every environment that's been set up. So, to enable and customise CloudWatch monitoring, we simply visit the CloudWatch section in the AWS Console.

By default, all the key metrics like CPU utilisation, memory, disk I/O and network traffic are available for every EC2 instance in our Beanstalk environment. Let's say we want to set up a basic CloudWatch alarm for high CPU usage. All we have to do is select "Alarms" in CloudWatch, create a new alarm and choose the relevant metric and threshold (e.g. "CPUUtilization > 80% for 5 minutes"). That way, we'll get alerts if our backend becomes overloaded or unresponsive. If we need to monitor something specific, like how many requests there are or custom health events, our Backend can be extended to send custom CloudWatch metrics using the AWS SDK. We can send metrics like "successful requests," "database errors," or "cache hits" straight to CloudWatch, so we can keep a really close eye on things. And, to set up a simple dashboard, we use the "Dashboards" feature in CloudWatch, add the metrics we want, and arrange them visually for continuous monitoring. These dashboards give us a quick overview of how our app is performing, so we can fix any issues straight away.

We make deployment a controlled, observable process by following these verification and monitoring steps. Every step, like accessing endpoints, reviewing health and logs, and setting up CloudWatch monitoring, tells us that our Backend is running smoothly, is robust and ready to handle real-world demand.

Updates, Rollbacks, and Scaling

Pushing Updates

After the initial deployment and successful monitoring, real-world projects always require updates, bug fixes, new features, or dependency upgrades. With AWS EB, pushing an update is streamlined and consistent. First, we make our changes in the codebase, rebuild the Docker image locally if necessary, and test it using the same procedure as during the initial containerization. Once the new version is verified, we commit the changes to our version control and ensure that all new artifacts (such as updated binaries, static assets, or configuration files) are present.

To deploy the updated application, we navigate to our project root and simply use the EB CLI:

```
eb deploy
```

From the above, the EB automatically uploads the new code, rebuilds the environment, and performs a rolling update, launching new instances with the updated version, verifying health, and then shifting traffic from old to new. Once deployed, we are able to verify the update using the same endpoint checks, dashboard reviews, and CloudWatch monitoring described earlier.

Performing Rollback

Sometimes, an update may cause unexpected errors, degraded performance, or even system outages. EB makes it possible to quickly roll back to a previous stable version without manual intervention. Through the AWS Management Console, we access the EB environment, and under the "Application versions" section, we find a history of previously deployed versions.

So here, to revert, we select a prior version and trigger a redeployment. The Beanstalk will re-launch the environment using that code and configuration. Alternatively, with the CLI, we can list available versions and use the following command to deploy a specific version:

```
eb list
eb deploy <version-label>
```

This immediate rollback capability ensures that the team can recover quickly from failed updates, restoring service and user trust while debugging the root cause offline.

Scaling Instances

As the user base grows or application traffic spikes, scaling becomes vital. EB environments can be scaled both vertically (by changing instance types for more CPU or memory) and horizontally (by increasing or decreasing the number of running instances). Horizontal scaling is managed automatically when environments are set up with load balancers, but manual scaling is also possible.

For example, if we want to adjust the number of instances, we can do it using the EB CLI:

```
eb scale 4
```

This command above instantly resizes the environment to run four EC2 instances. The AWS will handle provisioning, health checks, and load balancing, distributing incoming requests evenly across all running containers. Within the AWS Console, under the environment configuration, we can also set minimum and maximum instance counts, or configure automatic scaling triggers based on metrics like CPU or memory usage.

To sum up, all these post-deployment actions if we master it, we can certainly maintains a flexible, resilient backend. The updates are shipped confidently with the ability to roll back in seconds, and scaling ensures that performance remains steady, regardless of demand. All these practices combined together with continuous monitoring and automated deployment pipelines, simply contributes on one or the other to our robust backend project.

Summary

So, in this chapter, we got hands-on experience in turning our Backend project from a tested build into a fully deployed, production-ready service. The journey kicked off with a full deployment checklist, where we made sure everything was set for launch, including every configuration, environment variable, secret, database migration, and static asset. We got stuck in with containerisation, making a multi-stage Dockerfile that suited our project structure, then built and tested the Docker image locally to make sure it was reliable and consistent.

When we deployed on AWS EB, we got into the cloud, and we set up the EB CLI, configured environment variables and secrets, and ran our Dockerized backend with AWS-managed infrastructure. We also learned to track real-time metrics and set up alarms, making sure the service stayed strong and easy to see. At last, we looked at everything to do with the post-deployment lifecycle, like shipping updates with rolling deployments, doing rapid rollbacks if there were any errors, and scaling instances to match real-world demand. After getting the hang of these steps, we can easily create an easy-to-maintain and expandable deployment workflow for our Backend app.

Index

Epilogue

So far, you've gone through all the important stages of backend development, and you've seen how a simple project can grow into a system that's ready for production. The process of writing real C++23 backend code, configuring web servers, managing secrets, and troubleshooting live deployments is a great way to learn, even if you're not a fan of theoretical material. Each hands-on task has had a noticeable impact, reinforcing the habits that define skilled backend engineers. These include rigorous testing, thoughtful configuration, and a mindset of continuous improvement. Finishing this book is about way more than just getting to the last page. It's a sign that you've shifted from being a C++ programmer to being a solid backend developer, with a set of skills that are not only up to date but ready to take you into the future. Through these chapters, you've not only explored the mechanics of API design, containerization, deployment, and monitoring, but you've also got a way of thinking where you always build for reliability, clarity, and adaptability in fast-changing environments.

We've got some great principles here, like automated testing, stepwise deployment, modular architecture, and careful resource management. All of these are super important for high-quality software, but they're just the start. The tech, frameworks and best practices will keep on changing, and the backend landscape will see new patterns and tools pop up. But the confidence you gain from experience stays the same, so you can keep being curious and dedicated to your work. And as the world changes around us, the skills you gain here will stay with you for sure. It's possible you'll end up architecting more advanced distributed systems, implementing new protocols, or integrating cloud-native services that we only briefly touched on in these pages. The foundation we've laid makes those future steps seem less daunting and more exciting. The practical approach, incremental progress, and focus on understanding over rote memorisation will prepare you for roles and challenges that go well beyond this book.

The most important thing to remember is that backend engineering is all about curiosity and adaptability. Every project is different, and each one brings new challenges. As you refine your process, optimise for performance, or explore new libraries, remember that practical solutions are always within reach. If you keep experimenting and asking questions, and your backend systems show the same discipline and creativity you've encouraged here, then you'll be on to a winning formula.

I just wanted to say a quick thank you for choosing to take this journey and for trusting this book as your companion. What sets you apart is your persistence, focus and eagerness to learn. As you move forward, I hope every project will build on this foundation of reliability, security and constant improvement. The future of backend programming is bright, and you're more than ready to shape it.

Thank You

www.ingramcontent.com/pod-product-compliance
Lightning Source LLC
Chambersburg PA
CBHW061213240926
51846CB00006B/1216
9789349174566